KU-167-761

Stay Curious

LIBRARIES NI
WITHDRAWN FROM STOCK

Dedicated to Tony Davidson.
(It's all your fault)

Published by The Do Book Company 2018
Works in Progress Publishing Ltd
thedobook.co

Text copyright © Clare Hieatt 2018
Photography copyright © Individual photographs as listed on page 302

Endpaper artwork © Kate Sutton 2018

The right of Clare Hieatt to be identified as author of this work has been
asserted by her in accordance with the Copyright, Designs and Patents Act 1988

All rights reserved. No part of this publication may be reproduced, stored in or
introduced to a retrieval system, or transmitted in any form or by any means
(electronic, mechanical, photocopying, recording or otherwise) without the prior
written permission of the publisher. Requests for permission should be sent to:
info@thedobook.co

A CIP catalogue record for this book is available from
the British Library

ISBN 978-1-907974-47-2

Cover designed by Marion Deuchars
Book designed by Joby Barnard
Assistant designer Jordan Wright

Printed and bound by OZGraf Print on Munken,
an FSC-certified paper

5% of our proceeds from the sale of this book is given to
The Do Lectures to help it achieve its aim of making positive change:
thedolectures.com

1

Stay Curious

How We Created
a World Class Event
in a Cowshed

Clare Hieatt

BooK Co

Contents

The purpose of the Do Lectures is to give inspiring people a platform to share their stories with the hope that they will inspire others to do great things. It has been a beautiful and rewarding journey. To celebrate our 10th anniversary we have decided to share the story of Do in a book, in the hope that it might inspire others to create beautiful gatherings of their own.

Place

A sense of place

Do isn't easy. At the Do Lectures in Wales 2011, designer Frank Chimero did a talk about doing things 'the long, hard, stupid way' in reference to his own way of working and the greater sense of achievement that results. But it rang true with us. It could easily be a mantra for Do.

Do Wales is, at best, a five-hour journey from London. There's no easy way to get here. But when you do arrive, you feel that you have left your normal world behind. The setting of an old farm. The solidity of the stone buildings. The moss. The crows. The swallows. The wood smoke. The energy calms you. It grounds you. The journey is worth it.

For the Do Lectures held in the USA in the magical setting of Campovida, 90 minutes north of the Golden Gate Bridge, it's the same feeling. The gentle swish of the warm breeze through the ancient valley oaks, the dust on the paths, the abundance of the vegetable gardens, they immediately soothe and restore you.

So first, you have to make the journey. And when you arrive, you still face challenges that take you out of your comfort zone. You camp. You share a tent with strangers. You listen to people open up and share stories about themselves that move and inspire you. You rise early and go to bed late. You listen to rain on canvas. You see the stars. You dance. You laugh. You cry. You jump in a river or swim in the sea. You hug more people in that one weekend than you do in an entire year. You leave exhausted, but full.

The edge

The Do Wales Farm is on the far edge of west Wales. From here you can see the end of the River Teifi as it spills out into the Irish Sea. The alternative instructions on how to get here are: 'Leave London. Head west for five hours. Stop when you hit water.'

There's something to be said about being on the edge. The fringe. Being cut off from the mainstream. It's at the edge of places where interesting things tend to happen. Through economic necessity artists congregate at the edge of cities, being pushed further out as property value increases. At the forests' edge you find the flowers and plants that thrive in sunshine. There's also something courageous about being on the edge. Being in the bit between two worlds. Being the first to brave the storm (as we so often are here on the Welsh coast) before it makes its way inland, often losing force along its journey.

Being on the edge can also fill you with optimism. A daily reminder of being able to see the possibility of a different world. Space to think and dream. A large expanse of water reinforcing how vast the universe is and how insignificant your problems and worries are in comparison.

Although not overt or tangible, the feelings that are created by being in a place that is on the edge of somewhere are definitely woven into the fabric of the Do Lectures.

The farm, our home

Do Wales takes place on an old dairy farm overlooking Cardigan Bay. The history of the farm and surrounding land dates back to medieval times when the land was gifted to the first occupants by the monks of St Dogmael's Abbey. When we moved here, the old stone buildings which had once provided shelter to a large herd of British Friesians, had been empty for years. These buildings are slowly being reclaimed and given a new life as a home for the Do Lectures. The restoration is not one of painstakingly taking the buildings back to the way they were in an historical context, but more one of honouring their history by celebrating their repairs and adaptations over the years as working farm buildings. Concrete lintels, blockwork walls and corrugated metal roofing sits alongside old slate, lime mortar and fading limewash. We know that we are just passing through these buildings, and 'the home of the Do Lectures' is just the title given to one small chapter in its history. So we make sure that everything we are building inside them, can just as easily be taken away and the future generations of the barn owl family that live above the dining hall, will still be able to call this place home.

The farm is also our home. The farmhouse sits very close to the outbuildings. The gin bar is in our cellar. The new shower building has a laundry room on the back where we do our washing. The food in the vegetable garden feeds us all year round. The flowers that so beautifully decorate the many Do spaces occasionally make it on to our kitchen table as well. For us, this is what makes Do special. It's like having a large dinner party where all these amazing people come to your home and share their stories and give some much of themselves. We open up our home to them and they open up to us.

And because it's our home, we need some peace and quiet too. Do is not held in a venue that hosts a different event every weekend. It has a space that is unique to it; that can evolve with it and adapt to its needs. So much love and care can go into the preparation of the event, from the planting of the first seeds in the flower garden, to the building of a fire pit under the shelter of a tree, to the creation of toilet block with a place to brush your teeth with one of the best views of the bay. The Do Lectures is a special event because it has a home that is created especially for it.

'The setting, the format, the openness and the content make the Do unique. The Do Lectures portray the unconference experience. And it's because one is out of a comfort zone on so many levels, that one becomes receptive to all and everything during those four days'

Past attendee

'The Do Lectures has a humble vision to bring people together in 'hard-to-reach' places and let it all unfold.'

Past attendee

The first Do Lectures

The first Do Lectures was held at the magical Fforest Camp just a few miles from our farm. After a few years we were able to take it 'home' to nurture and sustain it, and to be able to host it in the heart of summer when there was a chance the sun would shine.

'It was the conversations in such an amazing space that really made the talks stay with me'

Past attendee

Tuesday company

The Do Lectures started as a 'Tuesday company'. The team would meet once a week on Tuesdays in what we call the Chicken Shed, which is in fact the old forge building on the farm. There's a small woodburner with a hotplate to boil a kettle and one electric radiator. As the team has grown and we have taken on more projects, the working days have increased (but the number of radiators hasn't), and Tuesday is still the day we all come together.

Work in progress

Each year we undertake a new project on the farm. We talk about it all through winter, start in spring and usually finish as the volunteers arrive to help us set up the event. The guiding principle behind all our work has been to create spaces that offer shelter but still feel like outdoor spaces. We have built simple structures within buildings to house the kitchen, toilets and showers, but we have left the other buildings as empty spaces so they can be used in different ways.

The cowshed

The talks are held in the 'beudy' (cowshed). We removed the stalls and added a polished concrete floor. We repaired where it was needed, but we left untouched all that we found beauty in; soft green moss-covered stone, fading limewash and peeling paint. We wanted to add to the story of the building, and not undo all that was done before.

If the walls could talk...

They would tell stories of feast and famine, flood and drought,
laughter and pain. They have provided shelter as generations of
farmers have worked the land. They have reverberated with the slow,
steamy breath of livestock settling into their straw beds for the night.
They have been a peaceful hunting-ground for silent barn owls and,
each spring they reawaken when the swallows return to raise their
young. And now, for a time, they have heard tales of passion, love
and endeavour as people have told their stories, their words resting in
the mortar and stone for generations to come.

Campovida

Our sister event, Do USA, takes place in Campovida in California. A family home, farm and business, surrounded by 500-year-old valley oaks and hillsides abundant with grapevines, with frosty, cold mornings that quickly become hot days. Campovida is just 90 minutes north of the Golden Gate Bridge, but it feels like a lifetime away.

'The Do Lectures hasn't just broken the
conference mould. It's turned it outside
in. Diverse, inclusive, unbranded, organic,
fluid, honest.'

Past attendee

There's something about seeing a circle of teepees set up beneath a sky full of stars on land that was once home to the Pomo Valley Indians that stops you in your tracks. The stories that were once told in this very place, the wisdom that was passed on through the generations that lived here, it feels right that this place is now home to a new generation of storytellers and wisdom sharers.

Abundance

We had a visitor to the farm a few years back. He had lived here as a boy. It was the end of summer and the trees in the orchard were heavy with fruit. He was surprised how much the place had changed now it wasn't a working farm. The word he used was 'abundance'. As a working farm, the land would have been well trodden, every space would have been used for animals or crops. But the land has had a rest for 15 years, nature has softened the edges and things have grown. It is so green here. Vivid, bright, vibrant. The upside of all the rain we get. Abundance is also a great word to describe the Do Lectures. It's full to bursting with inspiration and love and is a place where people feel compelled to give.

'The environment allows you
to be free and open, which
means it is impossible not to
connect.'

Past attendee

The 10 principles of place

1. Be in the middle of nowhere where it can be hard to get to.

2. Be somewhere where nature blows your mind.

3. Look for authenticity not perfection.

4. Blur the boundaries between indoors and outdoors.

5. Let the history be present.

6. Create a central hub where people can gather.

7. Provide quiet spaces.

8. Use materials from the locality.

9. Don't be rigid, let the space evolve and adapt.

10. Know when to stop.

'There is simply no way that the event would be the same run in a hotel or conference centre. The shared experience of camping, eating together and drinking beer together by the light of the fire pits lifted the whole event from the simply amazing to the truly magical.'

Past attendee

Curate

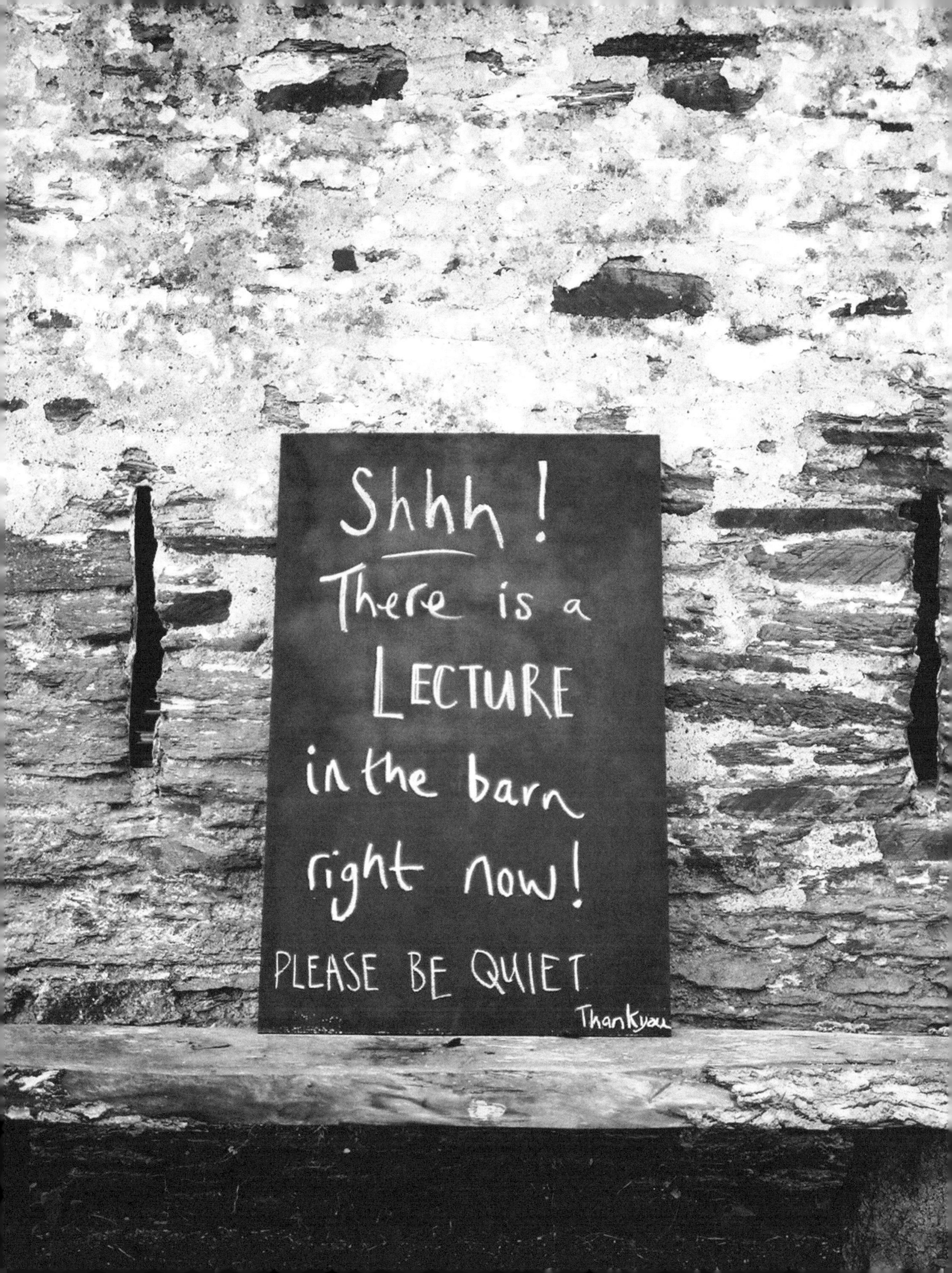
Shhh!
There is a
LECTURE
in the barn
right now!
PLEASE BE QUIET
Thankyou

The speakers

How we find our speakers

The central focus of the event is the talks. The Do Lectures was created to be a platform for inspiring people to share their stories in the hope that they will inspire others.

Researching and selecting speakers is the thing we spend most of our time on. Curating the right balance of messages and stories is an art. We have broad categories – design, business, food, wellbeing, sport, environment, tech, creativity – and we try to find people in these areas that are leading the way and making a positive difference. We don't always go for the obvious choices, we search out the mavericks, the risk takers or the ones who have taken an alternative path to get where they are.

There are some speakers who are on our list year after year. We write to them knowing that they will politely decline, in the hope that one day they might just say yes. Well, who wouldn't want David Attenborough talking in their cowshed?

'Doctors, designers, programmers, surfers, chefs, world travellers – the whole spectrum – they were all there. That diversity made the experience so rich, because we all came with something unique to contribute. This diversity sparked something unforeseen, gave the gathering a whole new life, as opposed to a normal conference – something that really couldn't be planned.'

Past attendee

**These simple sticks are nature's firestarters.
Light one and it will burn for hours.**

How come?

Well, they come from the stumps of pitch pine trees that were cut down at the turn of the century.
Their roots kept feeding the abandoned stumps with resin as if the whole tree was still there.
Every hour, every day for decades upon decades.

It's nature at its most combustible.

Touch them with your fingers and you can feel the wetness of the resin. Smell them and
you will think you are in an oil refinery. Boil them and you can make turpentine out of them.

It's a great story. And, no doubt, you will tell someone about it at some point. That's the thing
with stories. We like to pass them around. And the better the story, the more we tell it.

We think you have a great story. And we want you to come and tell it. So you can pass that
knowledge on. Like these sticks, you are a firestarter too. You remind the world of what is possible.
You light up people's imagination. You show them what they could be too.

The Do Lectures is an extraordinary world-renowned event that takes place in a barn, on a farm, on
the West Coast of Wales. It has proved life changing for the attendees, and indeed, for the speakers
too. It's a crazy mix of talks, workshops, music, comedy, art, running and jumping in the river.

There is nothing to compare it to. It's hard to describe, but even harder to leave. It's more of an
experience than an event. More like Burning Man mixed with Where The Wild Things Are.
No one leaves the same as they arrived.

We would love you to come light a fire at the Do Lectures (5-8th June 2014).

D. Hieatt ☺

David Hieatt Co-founder.

The speaker invitation

'We think you have a great story. And we want you to come and tell it. So you can pass that knowledge on. Like these sticks, you are a firestarter too. You remind the world of what's possible. You light up people's imagination. You show them what they could be too.'

How we brief our speakers

We ask speakers to do a talk they have never done before. To open up. To be vulnerable. We don't expect sleek over-rehearsed presentations and we don't offer speaker coaching. The best speakers are the ones who open up and tell their story in a natural way and talk from the heart. Often it's the speakers who are a little nervous or might be telling their story for the first time who deliver the best talks. Humility, vulnerability and honesty are the traits that really connect with the audience. Tears work too.

This is the brief we send to our speakers:

'Your talk.'

Do the talk you have always wanted to do, the one that scares you because it reveals the very essence of who you are.

We LOVE the hero's journey. The highs and the lows. And we LOVE vulnerability.

If there is a formula for DO talks, the ones that resonate most are those that are real, honest and powerful tales of human passion, resilience and compassion. They are human, humorous and humbling. And most of all, they make you feel that you could do something amazing too.

We get to see you as a human being. You allow us in.

Be human. Be you. Tell the story you have always wanted. If your voice shakes, it is because it matters.

'You will be reminded that the best communication is just storytelling and even though it's your story, others will recognise themselves in the narrative.'

Past attendee

A speaker's Do list

1. Tell your story. People want to see the human behind your story. Let them in.

2. Don't do the same old talk that you always do. It's time to leave your comfort zone.

3. Tell us of your struggles as well as your successes. Warts and all. Failure is often a better teacher than success.

4. Don't read it. Let it flow from the heart. You will touch more people that way.

5. Tell us your dreams, your passions, what you stand for. Tell us about your crazy new idea or your brave new thinking. We need to know what drives you.

6. Do entertain. We cover some serious subjects, but it doesn't mean it can't be fun. Entertainment is good. People learn a lot while laughing.

Ten years of talks

Andy Middleton
Do Founding Partner

Inspiration, learning, tears of joy and laughter. And ideas. So many ideas. Driving south from the Do Lectures to my home on the cliffs near St. Davids, I am full to the brim with possibilities and energised by friendship, deep conversations and hugs. Years after I first heard them, stories from barn, tent and fire pit resonate as strongly as the day they were shared. A testament to their depth and honesty.

The power of Do for me comes not from a single speaker but from the insistent and persuasive insights that return each year, freshly told by travellers' journeys of discovery – different but similar. Whether the experiences at the Do Lectures are seen through the lens of Joseph Campbell's Hero's Journey, or one of Christopher Booker's seven basic stories, it's the clarity of those repeating themes that have helped me shape and deliver ideas for a better world. Here are some ideas that have stuck for good:

Keep ambition wild.

Nicky Spink's casual telling of her Double Bob Graham Round, an astounding 122-mile run with 54,000 feet of climbing, rewrote the rules of possibility beyond the age of 50. Listening to the power of Daniel Epstein's dreams of change five years ago, and having the pleasure of supporting 'Unreasonable' businesses today, show clearly why outrageous goals help us do our best work.

Let your story unfold.

Paul Sinton-Hewitt's parkrun, Joshua Coombes' 'Do Something for Nothing' and C.J. Bowry's Sal's Shoes were beautifully told tales of ideas that were given space and time to grow. Fuelled by conviction and values, but unforced, their projects have changed the world.

Make your own rules.

It's no surprise that Do attracts participants and speakers who carve their own paths. Bill Drummond, Sarah Corbett, Mr Bingo, all taught me that outliers have the most fun and impact, and that the more we wear difference as a gift, not a challenge, the easier it is for others to welcome it, and us.

Build better tools.

Gabriel Branby's compelling obsession with quality has rung true with every split of 10,000 hardwood logs that I've made with my Gränsfors Bruks axes. Anna Young's ability to help users become makers through MakerHealth leaves an itch unscratched for me to bring her know-how to Wales. And Floyd Woodrow's Compass for Life will bring hope to a million young minds as we help kids find their own reason for learning.

Listen to your heart.

David and Alison Lea-Wilson's tales of salt and ocean enterprise at Halen Môn are complemented by Darina Allen's mission to help people fall in love with place, land and food through her programmes at Bally-maloe. Al Humphreys' shift from Arctic exploration to micro-adventures, driven by a call from heart and home, is one that we can all listen to more closely.

My annual pilgrimage to the Do Lectures, and times catching up with the Cardigan crew and Doers around the world throughout the year, are opportunities to drink from the firehose of hope, know-how and optimism. When challenges come my way, stories and connections from Do are the best keys I could wish for to unlock new doors of possibility.

Cheryl Strayed

'Into the wild. Into the body. Out of the mind.'

Do USA, 2012

Tim Ferriss

'Be strategically unreasonable.'

Do Wales, 2008

Perry Chen

'99% of ideas are not conceived to gencrate revenue.'

Do Wales, 2011

Peter Farrelly

'Chasing your dream is all about love. That's it, love.'

Do USA, 2014

Zach Klein

'Build the company that you wouldn't sell.'

Do Wales, 2013

Holley Murchison

'Own your voice.'

Do Wales, 2016

Michael Acton Smith

'Keep the main thing, the main thing.'

Do Wales, 2013

Marion Deuchars

'Teenagers are past the age of learning to draw,
and close to the age of remembering to draw.'

Do Wales, 2012 & Teen Do, 2016

Anna Jones

'What and how I eat defines how my body and mind feels.'

Do Wales, 2015

Sir Tim Berners-Lee

'We're very much connected. Our jobs depend on this web thing.'

Do Wales, 2010

Talks that changed me

Mark Shayler
Do Founding Partner

Each year at the Do Lectures there are stand-out talks. And each year there are talks that don't stand out until after I've gone home and thought about them.

But every year I'm changed by the event. Sometimes a little, and sometimes in a big way. I can't think of a bad Do Lecture and have really struggled to identify the one talk that changed me. I could give you my top ten; I could even filter it down to my top four:

Mickey Smith
Steve Edge
James Alexander
Sean Carasso

But I can only have one. So, I'm going to choose the one that moved me the most, that still makes me cry, and that resonates with me most days. I'm going to choose Sean Carasso.

'How to fight a war with a whistle'
Sean Carasso

I was lucky enough to be chairing this session. I wasn't supposed to be. It was the very last lecture on the last day. One of the other founding partners had been allocated the slot but due to one reason or another he couldn't do it. I'd read about Sean and, at the time, I was working on the circular economy and the use of rare-earths in electronics, so I leapt at the chance to host this one.

Sean started gently. He told us about growing up in California, about sharpening his entrepreneurial skills selling glow sticks at festivals to stoned ravers, about having to do so to play his part in keeping the family going. He told us about success as his family pioneered quinoa growing. He told us about travelling the world partying. He told us about coming down from the party with a bang when he woke up in the Democratic Republic of the Congo. If you have to add the words 'democratic' and 'republic' to the name of a country then you can be certain it is neither of these things.

He was playing football with some kids. Kids with guns. Boy soldiers. Sean was shocked. They explained it was normal. It was life (and sometimes death). They explained they were lucky, because they had guns. The young kids had only whistles. Their job was to make as much noise as possible on the frontline to put the opposition off their shot. They usually died.

Sean was understandably alarmed. Then he did what every white middle-class person would do: he wrote a blog. He called it 'Falling Whistles'. The response was massive. He flew home. Got drunk at his home-coming party and ranted. He ranted about how the boy soldiers were protecting mines. Mines that produced the elements that make the components to make our phones that make us happy. The things that kill them make us happy. We are all connected. Two things happened. Sean didn't get invited to many more parties. And he set up a charity called Falling Whistles.

Do Auction

Sean moved the audience to tears. I will always remember looking up from tweeting about how incredible this story was (oh the irony) and seeing the veins standing proud in Sean's neck. Seeing the passion, love and anger mixed together in the sweat on his brow. I hugged him afterwards and he tried to give me the whistle round his neck, the whistle his charity sold to raise money to create enterprise and change in a country that had never needed it so badly. I thanked him but said no. I said we would auction it at the Do Auction after the talks. Then I had to compose myself as I am the auctioneer.

David and Clare agreed that 50% of the money raised at the auction would go to Falling Whistles. We raised £26,000. That's ace. And nearly everyone there went home and bought a whistle from Sean's website. That's ace. But Sean's story stayed with me. I tell his story every month or so. Every time I talk about what we make and why we make it. I think about his story every time my phone is due an upgrade, every time I see an advert saying: 'upgrade early' or 'our new 3D curved TV will make you happier'. I think about the boys – the brothers, sons, grandsons – protecting those mines. I think about the sisters brutalised by a culture of war, a culture of rape. I think about the mothers and fathers who will never see their sons grow up.

The thing that makes us happy harms them.

The Do Lectures matter. They find untold stories and they change everyone that attends. They have changed me.

Watch Sean's talk: thedolectures.com

Talks that changed me

Clare Hieatt
Co-founder

'How the human family can do better'
Maggie Doyne

Maggie Doyne, a 23-year-old fresh-faced American, got on the stage at Do Wales in 2012 and told the story of how she took a gap year to travel the world before going to college. She never made it to college but instead ended up becoming 'Mom' to 30 orphaned Nepalese kids and now she was building a school to educate many more. It was one of the most moving talks I have listened to at the Do Lectures and the one I always reference when people ask me which talks they should watch online.

When I was giving birth to my first child at 32, I cried out the words 'I'm too young to be a mother' (these words were actually recorded in my birth notes by the midwife) in the desperate hope that my daughter might decide to give me a few more months to get used to the idea of motherhood. You see, I was questioning whether I would be any good at it. Perhaps I needed to read a few more books, attend more ante-natal classes, ask more questions of my friends who were already parents. And this attitude of questioning, talking myself out of things, thinking that other people would be better, more qualified or experienced than me, was something that had been slowing my decision making and dulling my instinct for years.

But there was Maggie, a young woman and mum to 30, on stage telling her story. She was passionate. She was emotional. But what struck me most was her naivety. She achieved what she did *because* she was young. She didn't question whether she was able to adopt these kids because she hadn't been an adult long enough to be conditioned into thinking she couldn't. She didn't worry about red tape, or legalities, or insurance, or liabilities, she just got on with it and made it happen. It was humbling. I don't think it was just me who felt it. I think there were a lot of people who were questioning what they had done with their lives and whether they would ever have the courage to Do, as Maggie had done.

I remember asking myself: had I seen Maggie do that talk when I was 16 years old, would I have trodden a different path? Would I have gone out into the world and made a huge difference to the lives of many?

Maggie's talk didn't necessarily change me. It moved me and inspired me. And it influenced the way I encourage my daughters to question how they can make a difference. But if my 16-year-old self had had the chance to hear Maggie's story, well she would have been a very different person. I like to think that she would have forged her path and gone into the world inspired and ready to make change. Without doubt. Without question.

Watch Maggie's talk: thedolectures.com

Talks that changed me

Carlo Navato
Do Founding Partner

'Do trust in the things you love'
Mickey Smith

Mickey Smith changed everything for me.

Mickey is a surfer, a photographer, and a musician. But more than that, Mickey is a maker of visual and sonic landscapes. A student of nature and a philosopher.

When I responded to David and Clare's invitation to support the Do Lectures mission back in 2008, I did so because of Mickey Smith. I hadn't met him then, I'd never actually heard of him to be honest. But I had a hunch that the Do Lectures was all about the Mickey Smiths of the world.

You see, Mickey has a story that has to be shared. Not because he's famous (although he certainly is in the cold-water surfing community), but because he's an exceptional man.

Mickey grew up in west Cornwall, a place of outstanding wild and rugged beauty. A place he describes as being full of natural goodness and off-the-wall, crazy, lovely people. For anyone who's visited, this is a place that easily ranks as a jewel in the UK's crown.

But west Cornwall has a darker side. It's a story of diminished and dying industries, a lack of opportunity, and of outsiders appropriating the best housing. A place Mickey has described as dead, with unemployed fishermen and miners fighting for scraps. It's a place where locals like Mickey can feel hopeless, like second class citizens or strangers in their own towns. And that was the story that was drummed into Mickey as he grew up. The story that west Cornwall had nothing to offer him.

But Mickey was a kid who always had a smile on his face. When a change in family circumstances meant upheaval, he spent a love-filled summer on the beaches and in the sea off Land's End. He drifted and floated on pieces of wood and plastic – whatever he could find. He was nurtured by the love and shared laughter of his mum and sister.

When Mickey started playing every musical instrument he could lay his curious hands on, and began gigging in pubs, clubs and festivals around Cornwall, his perception shifted. Life was not all doom and gloom. Driven by a desire to live creatively, Mickey was able to start earning a living pursuing his passions: music, photography, film making and surfing.

Living on the road, hand to mouth, sleeping on floors, in vans, and on beaches, Mickey learned his trade. And his work started to get noticed.

Magazines wanted to publish his photography and the surfing fraternity wanted to commission his cinematography. Because his work was a rare thing: It was made with soul. An extraordinary soul that has a humility and an integrity that comes from a deep love and respect. It was a love for the wild, life-giving force of the ocean in all its moods and colours. And a respect for its awesome power and unpredictability.

Mickey spent countless hours surfing in waters all around the world. He shared tales and built unshakeable bonds with people from all walks of life. Always open-minded, always ready to glimpse the magic around him. His creative work was suffused with a quality and sincerity that just can't be faked.

The Dark Side of the Lens, a film Mickey made to explain his work to his sister Cherry, received a rapturous response when he played it at the end of his Do Lecture in 2011. It's the most beautiful, powerful and poignant 6 minutes of visual storytelling I've ever seen. It brought me and countless others to tears. Mickey's response to the raucous applause and cheering? He grinned, giggled, hung his head and humbly said, 'Thanks guys, thanks a lot.'

Mickey summed up his life philosophy for the Do Lectures audience. Arm yourself with a grin, embrace being out of control and let your weirdness flow free. Trust in the things you love, get primal with nature and take time to experiment and learn new things. Trust your instincts and run with them always. Use your fears and failures as fuel for the onward journey.

Mickey finished with an exhortation. Do what you love for a living he said, but be wise – don't let the pursuit of money kill your enthusiasm for what you love.

The Dark Side of the Lens is dedicated to his sister Cherry who sadly passed away. The film is bathed in a mournful quality. In it, he makes a confession. 'If I only scrape a living, at least it's a living worth scraping. If there's no future in it, this is a present worth remembering.'

Mickey Smith will not go to his grave wondering what could have been.

Mickey Smith changed everything for me. His talk shone a bright light on the visceral power of humility and the need for authenticity. His philosophy is one I shared with my kids immediately afterwards.
He is everything I hoped the Do Lectures could be. He is a king of life.

I celebrate you, Mickey Smith, Lord of the Waves.

Watch Mickey's talk: thedolectures.com

Talks that changed me

Anna Beuselinck
Co-founder Do USA

'A changed man'
James Alexander

We came to find James Alexander through a connection to another Do Lectures speaker, Maggie Doyne. Like Maggie, James had received the Hero of Compassion Award from the Dalai Lama. And when we called to ask him if he might speak at the Do Lectures, his warmth and smile came through the phone.

As James began his talk, a collective silence descended and the barn was filled with acceptance and understanding. James shared his journey from incarceration to freedom with such honesty. He displayed a depth of courage and commitment that the audience responded to with both compassion and hope.

His willingness to relive the difficult parts of his journey with such intimacy led to a question and answer session after the talk. Another speaker, Peter Farrelly, was in the audience and asked James a very poignant question. James burst into tears, which moved the entire audience. We became united through his story. We were one in our humanity. The Do Lectures provides this kind of experience which is hard to put into words or capture on film.

James Alexander, Do USA 2014

Watch James' talk: thedolectures.com

The attendees

We provide a space for magic to happen, but the magicians are the people who attend.

The attendees are as important to the Do Lectures as the speakers. Often they are as inspiring and have as many great stories to tell.

Over the years the number of people wanting to attend has grown, but we are limited by how many people we can fit in the old cow barn. So we invite people to apply for tickets. We have a very informal list of questions that help us get to know what the potential attendees are like; what they are interested in, what they are passionate about and where they are in their lives. This helps us gather a diverse group of attendees; people who are from different backgrounds, but who are united by like-minded thinking. And this is what makes the Do Lectures so special. The limited size of the facilities ensures that the event will always be small and intimate. Over the course of the weekend you get to meet most of the people. Even though you might attend alone, you definitely leave feeling like you belong to the Do community.

Each year we strive to get better, not bigger.

'It's rare in life that you get
to spend a few intimate days
with people from a different
background to you, who
do a different job to you,
who might come from a
completely different culture
to you and you realise that
beneath all the layers of
status, business and background, you are the same.
You discover that your tribe
might not be your family or
the people you work with,
but the small group of
people you met in a barn
in the middle of nowhere.'

Past attendee

Workshops

The Do Lectures isn't just about listening, it's also about doing. The days start with (optional) physical workshops, and after lunch there are also practical workshop sessions.

For those who like an early start, there's the option to join a yoga session on the deck, go for a run along the estuary, or take a swim in the sea.

The afternoon workshops focus on a practical skill, a welcome antidote to the intensity of listening to the talks, and to give people a chance to switch off and try their hand at something they might never have experienced before.

Ten years of learning through doing: Bread baking, film making, choir singing, business building, dumpling making, rabbit skinning, fermenting, paper cutting, jam making, wine tasting, drumming, photographing, storytelling, life planning, vision boarding, magazine publishing, death facing, illustrating, lino printing, log chopping, breathing, music video making, fire cooking, T-shirt printing, star gazing.

**James from Otter Surfboards
runs a hand plane workshop.**

'Rimming': a new sport invented at The Do Lectures, consisting of a muddy run/jog along the banks of the river Teifi followed by a swim/ paddle where the river meets the sea at Poppit Sands beach.

Day 1, everyone signs up.

Day 2, the numbers are halved.

Day 3, it's a solitary experience.

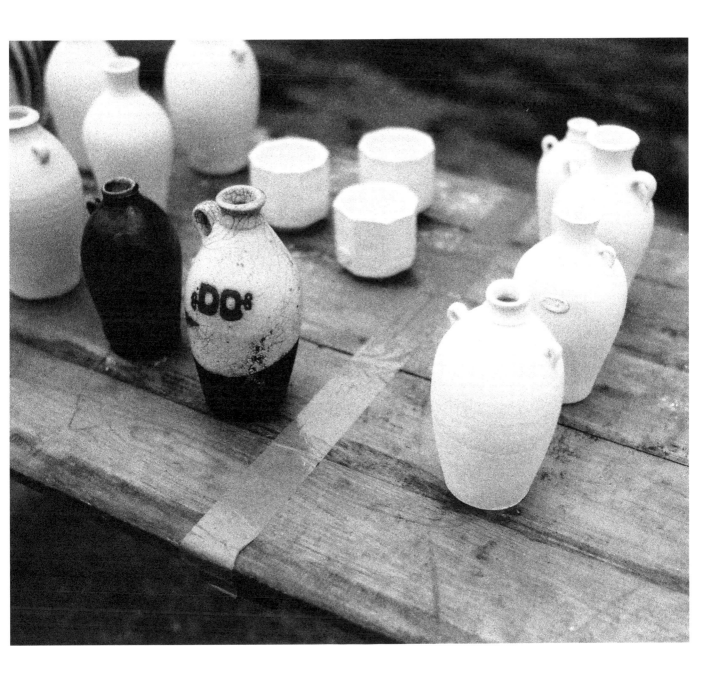

'The unique environment of Do is an essential part of why it gets underneath your skin so comprehensively. You're immersed in every aspect of it.'
Past attendee

In the midst of doing, find time to be

by Michael Townsend Williams

Everyone at Do is challenging themselves somehow. To run the best event they can. To finally start that business. To create the work they always dreamed of. To give the talk of their lives.

Early morning at Do, a number of them wake up, leave their tents behind and make their way onto the deck for yoga, breathing and meditation. Shaking off train rides, car shares and, for some, long-haul flights too. Some are seasoned yogis, others finally taking their first step. Everyone excited, yet at the same time in need of calm for the day ahead.

All share the need to reconnect their minds and bodies. And that connection is found through their breath, and by being fully present. For the best Doers also know how to be.

What we do

Lying down, we open out our legs and arms, and turn our palms upward. This position can make us feel vulnerable, so we ground ourselves by being aware of all the points of contact between our bodies and the earth beneath us.

We listen, with our eyes closed, to sounds around us – the starlings, the distant traffic, that noisy group of runners ... We notice our bellies rising and falling with our breath ... We start to stretch and wake up our bodies.

Before moving on to the yoga asanas, we practise some yogic breathing exercises (see page 100) to release tension and help us feel calm and centred.

We remind ourselves to connect with our bodies and our feelings.
(We are all so much more than that 5 per cent of our brain that 'thinks'.)

Moving slowly and then a little faster – always with awareness of our breath – we begin: A few rounds of sun salutations that use pretty much every muscle in the body; then some classical positions – shoulder stands, forward and backward bends, side stretches and long deep twists – that work on all the systems of the body to bring them back into balance.

We stop, relax and do nothing for a while.

And then we sit together for some quiet time ... Set an intention to ourselves for the day ahead ... And remember a few things to be thankful for in our lives, here and now.

To know even one life has breathed
easier because you have lived.
This is to have succeeded.

Ralph Waldo Emerson

There are two simple things we focus on.

1. **Awareness**

If you cannot control where your attention goes, how can you expect to control the direction of your life or business? Self-awareness can be improved through mindful practise and focusing on what you are feeling while you are doing. It is the ability to relate to the feelings and sensations of being fully alive in the present moment. Living with more self-awareness allows you to make better choices.

2. **Relaxation**

So many of us are over-stimulated. We have lost the ability to deeply relax mentally and physically. And yet this is what makes us more resilient – better placed to cope with challenges and recover from them. By lengthening our exhalations we learn how to relax more quickly and deeply.

So next time you have a lot to do, don't forget to be. A little bit of yoga every morning can make a lot more happen later.

Yogic breathing exercises

Belly breathing

Lie down on your back. If you find it uncomfortable, raise your knees with your feet on the floor. Place both hands on your belly. Now try to breathe in and out through the nose, making your hands rise and fall with your belly. If your chest continues to move as you breathe, place a hand on the chest and press down firmly to encourage you to use the belly more.

So as you breathe in, the belly rises. As you breathe out, the belly falls (draw your belly down towards the floor). Breathe in and out through the nose. Count to four as you breathe in and count to six as you breathe out.

Kapalabhati

Kapalabhati (literal meaning – shining skull) are rhythmic exhalations with a pumping action that flush out your lungs of old air, stimulate the nervous system and release tension. Sit cross-legged or kneeling with your back straight.

Take three deep in-and-out breaths to prepare. Then draw your tummy in sharply as you exhale. Repeat the exhalations once every second so you get into a rhythm. Don't hold your breath. You will be inhaling but not consciously. Just focus on the sharp exhalations. If you find this difficult try placing your hand on your tummy and press gently with each exhalation. It can take time for your stomach muscles to react quickly enough. This exercise is only possible after you have mastered belly breathing. Repeat with 20 pumps at first and then breathe deeply and hold your breath for 30 seconds if possible. This is one round. Repeat three rounds. You can build up the repetitions from 20 to 30 to 40 to 60. You can also learn to retain your breath for longer as well. Don't be too competitive though. Slow steady progress is best.

Alternate nostril breathing

Create a focused, calm, flow state by balancing your autonomic nervous system with alternate nostril breathing. When you breathe through your right nostril, your sympathetic response (fight or flight–the stress response) is activated. When breathing through your left nostril, your parasympathetic response (rest and digest – the relaxation response) is activated.

Sit with your back straight. Close your right nostril with your right thumb and exhale through the left nostril. Inhale through the left nostril, close it with your right ring finger and exhale through the right. Inhale through the right nostril, close it with your thumb and exhale through the left.

And repeat. Try to do this for three minutes, counting to three with each breath. In time increase the count to five. Six breath cycles per minute is, for most people, an optimum rate to positively affect your physiology.

Sun salutations

One round of sun salutation consists of two sequences, the first leading with the right foot in positions 4 and 9, the second leading with the left. Keep your hands in one place from positions 3 to 10 and try to co-ordinate your movements with your breathing. Start by practising four rounds and gradually build up to twelve rounds.

Exhaling, lower your knees, then your chest and then your forehead, keeping your hips up and your toes curled under.

Inhaling, lower your hips, point your toes and bend back. Keep legs together and shoulders down. Look up.

Inhaling, stretch your arms forward, then up and back over your head and bend back slowly from the waist, as in position 2.

Exhaling, gently come back to an upright position and bring your arms down by your sides.

Stand with feet together and hands in the prayer position in front of your chest. Make sure your weight is evenly distributed. Exhale.

Inhaling, stretch your arms up and arch back from the waist, pushing the hips out, legs straight. Relax your neck.

Exhaling, fold forward, and press your palms down, fingertips in line with toes – bend your knees if necessary.

Retaining the breath, bring the other leg back and support your weight on hands and toes.

Diagram courtesy of the Sivananda Yoga Vedanta organisation.

Dan Rubin runs a portrait
photography workshop

'We don't regret the thing
we tried and failed at, we
regret the thing we never
attempted.'

Paul Deegan, Do Wales 2009

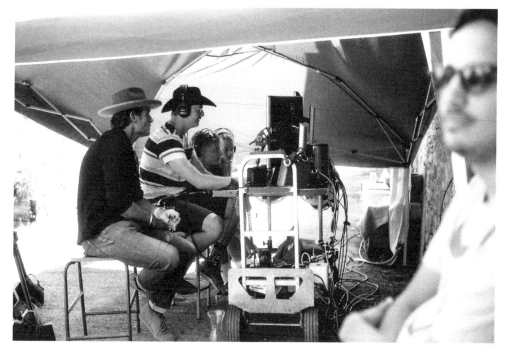

Do Live Streaming: The last two Do Lectures events have been live streamed, making them available to an audience far bigger than the cowshed could ever hold. We've heard stories of people putting on their own mini Do events and inviting friends to watch the live streaming with them.

The Giving Chair

In the early days, some of the friends of the Do Lectures would buy tickets to the event knowing full well they were unable to attend, but their generosity enabled us to give free places away and still have the funds to keep the event going. This is how the Giving Chair was born. The kindness has continued over the years with past attendees wanting to fund places for students. So every year we have a number of free places to give away; all we ask is that the lucky recipient makes a short film of their experience to say thank you to the person who gave them the place.

Teen Do

Our daughters, Stella and Tessa, have been lucky enough to attend every Do Lectures event in Wales and also a few of the California ones as well. All year round the conversation at our dinner table flits from who said what at school, to who said yes to doing a talk. It has been as much a part of their lives as it has ours. While we might get overexcited at the prospect of Radiohead's Colin Greenwood doing a talk in our barn, they just seem to take it all in their stride.

One such dinner conversation resulted in us agreeing that they could hold their own Do Lectures event for teenagers, on the condition that they did most of the planning, promotion and curation of the event. So, with a small team of friends, that is exactly what they did.

The first Teen Do was in August 2016, the second in July 2017. The teen team researched and booked all their speakers, plus they managed to get some of their heroes to speak. They promoted the event through social media and they planned and scheduled all the talks and workshops. The food was even cooked by a talented team of teenage chefs. We just did the clearing up!

Teen Do was one of my best Do experiences. Seeing a group of young strangers open up and be generous and loving towards each other, and talk and share with such awareness and wisdom, gave me hope that the future is safe in their hands.

'The other teens there were so welcoming
and lovely, and the sense of community
that developed in just that one weekend
was wonderful.'

Past attendee

Detail

Do is in the detail

You know when you walk into a space for the first time and you immediately feel at home? What is it about those special places that make you feel like you belong as soon as you walk through the door?

More often than not it's the little details that show that your comfort has been considered and your needs cared for. A pitcher of water at your bedside. A flickering candle on the kitchen table. A comfy seat by a crackling fire.

That's what we try to create at the Do Lectures. Most people arrive on their own after a long journey. We get that they are probably feeling a little apprehensive about meeting new people, sharing a tent and having dinner with strangers. So, we greet them with a big smile and a whole lot of carefully considered details to make them feel welcome.

From the lush abundance of the ferns, the smell of stacked apple wood and the flickering of candles that greet you as you check in. The freshly roasted coffee, the carefully brewed teas and the delicious cakes where you mingle and meet your fellow attendees.

The smell of food cooking over coals. Meals in the candle lit barn that warm and nourish you. The candles that light the path back to your tent. The hot water bottle and tea making station lit up like a beacon in the camp at night. The bunches of lemon balm and mint tied to the shower-heads and the stack of soft, fresh towels to dry yourself with. Brushing your teeth looking at a view of the bay. And what a view it is: it seriously fills your heart with joy.

You might come to the Do Lectures and not notice any of these things. But you will get a sense of feeling welcome and cared for. For us, these details are extremely important. We have conversations with our log suppliers about which wood smells best when it burns. We stock our vegetable garden with flowers that will burst into bud on the very weekend of Do (always a risk with our unpredictable weather). We make sure everyone has a candle burning outside their tent to welcome them back at night.

'If it was comfortable, there would be no point. If it was a day like any other we'd be less inspired, less excited and less likely to be innovative'

Past attendee

Food

Our food is made with love. No doubt about it. Our cooks are passionate about what they do and nothing gives them more pleasure than creating delicious comforting meals for everyone.

Mealtimes are important at Do. We all sit together on long communal tables and eat the same food. It's like a family meal. And that's the way we like it.

Mealtimes provide a welcome pause between the intensity of the talks. They give people a chance to relax and spend time chatting to fellow attendees, speakers, or volunteers. There are no name badges or table settings. Just good honest food and good honest conversation. One thing we always notice is that the noise volume in the dining barn increases as the weekend progresses.

In west Wales we are lucky to have amazing ingredients right on our doorstep. Great fish, meat and vegetables can all be sourced from a few miles away. We grow salads and herbs in our vegetable garden right outside our kitchen.

In Campovida, the humble kitchen garden is taken to another level. Rows and rows of the most delicious vegetables ripen in the California sunshine, in a garden you can wander through and get lost in.

Ken, who tends the garden, will take you on a walk, glass of homemade wine in hand, and pick things for you to try that will complement the wine you're drinking.

The magic happens in the space between the talks – and a lot of that is at mealtimes.

Legendary meals at Do

1. Anja's beetroot crumble. A meal served back in the day when Do was held on a wet April weekend at Fforest camp. Warm, comforting, wholesome. Who knew a single vegetable could be so fulfilling?

2. Mimi's breakfast granola. A wonderful way to wake up after a night under the stars at Do USA.

3. Jen's lamb curry. Delicious and hearty with so many super tasty chutneys and accompaniments.

4. Eduardo and Ranga's Sri Lankan mussels at Do USA. Fresh out of the sea, cooked to perfection, served with cold beer.

5. Bertha's sourdough pizza. The most tasty pizza ever, cooked in a wood-fired oven in the back of a Land Rover. It has become a tradition for the last meal of Do Wales.

Beetroot crumble

Anja Dunk
Serves 6

When planning the food for the very first Do Lectures, it didn't occur to me that some people might not like beetroot. I wrote the menu up on the chalkboard. On reading 'Beetroot Crumble', the first person in line held out his plate and asked for the other option. I replied there wasn't one. 'But I don't like beetroot,' he said. And he wasn't alone.

Luckily, though, despite a few grumbles, the handful of beetroot haters were good sports and at least willing to give it a go. By the time we had finished serving, a little queue of people lining up for seconds had formed, and guess who was standing in it? 'Can I have the recipe?' he said, holding up his plate a second time.

Ingredients

1kg cooked beetroot, sliced into ½ cm-thick rounds
300g mature cheddar, grated
500ml single cream
2 cloves garlic, crushed
2tsp fresh thyme leaves
1tsp fine sea salt
120g fresh breadcrumbs

Method

Preheat the oven to 200°C/180°C fan.

Layer half of the beetroot in a large gratin dish, then sprinkle with 100g of the grated cheddar, followed by another layer of the remaining beetroot slices. Mix the cream, garlic, thyme and salt together in a jug and pour this over the beetroot. Mix the rest of the cheddar with the breadcrumbs and sprinkle on top.

Bake in the centre of the oven for 25 minutes until golden brown on top and bubbling at the sides. Serve with a sharply dressed green salad and a loaf of crusty bread.

Breakfast granola

Mimi Beaven
Makes approx. 16 servings

This granola started with a recipe from my friend Heidi who was my right hand at Do USA in 2011 and 2012. It's really easy to adapt by switching out the fruits, nuts and seeds for alternatives. The oil and sweeteners can also be varied too.

Ingredients

125g seeds – a mix of sunflower and pumpkin seeds
500g rolled oats
175g coconut shreds or flakes
150g chopped nuts – walnuts, hazelnuts, pistachios or almonds
165g honey or maple syrup

100g olive or coconut oil – or a more neutral canola or sunflower oil
450g dried fruit – a mix of figs and raisins works well but you could use one fruit or a blend of several: currants, sultanas, dates, prunes, apricots, cherries or cranberries
25g flax and/or sesame seeds

Method

Preheat the oven to 160°C.

Place the seeds (not including the flax/sesame seeds) on a lined baking tray and toast in the oven for about 5 minutes. Set aside to cool. Mix the oats, coconut and chopped nuts in a large bowl. Whisk together the oil and the honey (or maple syrup) then pour into the oat mixture. Combine until well blended.

Place the coated oats evenly on a lined baking tray, making sure the layer is not too deep. Use two trays if necessary. Place in the preheated oven and bake for 10 mins rotating the trays to brown evenly. If the edges are turning brown quickly, stir to bring the outside edges in. Bake for a further 20 mins, checking after 10 mins and then every 5 until everything is golden brown. The granola will continue to crisp as it cools. As soon as you take it out of the oven sprinkle the flax and/or sesame seeds evenly over the hot granola. This will ensure they stick. If you wait until the granola cools, they will all end up in the bottom of the granola jar.

When the granola has cooled down, add the dried fruit and combine before putting it in an airtight container. Use within 3-4 weeks.

Lamb curry

Jen Goss
Feeds 6-8

I love a good curry, there's always something for everyone and it's a real feast to be shared – my favourite kind of meal. Whenever we cook curry at Do it's always a huge success. This curry is even better if you have time to make it the day before to allow the spices to mingle for even longer.

Ingredients

2 medium onions
4 cloves garlic
3cm ginger
3tbsp sunflower oil
3tsp ground cumin
3tsp ground coriander
2 sticks cinnamon
4 whole cardamom pods

½ tsp chilli powder
1½ tsp ground turmeric
1 kilo diced lamb shoulder
3 x 400g tins chopped tomatoes
2tbsp greek yoghurt
300g cleaned spinach or chard
2tsp garam masala
Small handful chopped coriander

Preheat the oven to 170ºC/Gas mark 4.

Method

Peel the onion, garlic and ginger and blend into a paste in a food processor. In a casserole dish or heavy bottom pan that has a tight fitting lid, heat the oil and fry the onion paste for 5 minutes. Add the spices and fry for another 2 minutes.

Add the lamb and coat with the spicy paste and fry for 2 minutes. Add the tomatoes and bring to a simmer. When gently bubbling, cover and put in the oven for 2 hours. Stir after the first hour and check the liquid, if it feels dry add 50ml water.

After 2 hours the meat will be nice and tender, add the yoghurt and stir. Then add the spinach and stir again, it will cook in the residual heat. Season with salt and pepper. Stir in the garam masala. Garnish with coriander.

Serve with basmati rice, dahl, poppadoms, raita and a selection of pickles and chutneys and a nice cold glass of beer.

Sourdough-it-all

Tom Herbert
Makes one sourdough loaf

A couple of years ago I made a scaled up version of this dough for an afternoon Bread Workshop at the Do Lectures. Several hours later and well after midnight, the risen dough was placed into the much-cooled Bertha's pizza oven on the back of a Land Rover. I was 'helped' by Ian Matthews, the inquisitive and hungry drummer from Kasabian. Once this behemoth of a loaf was baked, I carried it into the Secret Gin Bar where it was announced, held aloft and passed round – steaming as it was broken – filling the intimate and lively space with the best smell in the world.

Ingredients
4 cups (480g) strong white bread flour,
plus extra for dusting
1 cup (280g) sourdough starter
1 cup hot or cold water
Big pinch (10g) of sea salt

This recipe is a great catch-all bread recipe that works in many varied ways: Pizza, flatbreads, pitta, or a whole sourdough loaf.

Preheat the oven to 230°C.

Method
Add the ingredients to a bowl and mix together. Only add more water or flour if you're really sure you need it.

No skimping on the kneading. Take it slow for a full 15 minutes. Once your dough is smooth and soft, put it back in the bowl, cover, and leave it somewhere warm to rise for 2 hours.

After that, take your dough out and shape it on a very lightly floured surface and pop into a basket or tin. Again, cover and leave somewhere warm to rise. If you've used hot water this will need 4 hours' rising. Bake your bread at 230°C and dropping to 210°C after 10 minutes or so. Starting off hot gives a good spring; lowering the heat gives a thorough bake. Bake time is likely to be around 35 to 40 minutes (check after 20 minutes). To check it's fully baked hold the loaf with a dry cloth or glove and tap the bottom. If it sounds hollow, it's baked!

How to lay a Do dinner table

Meals at Do are relaxed and informal. There are no seating plans. There are no reserved spaces. The food is served at serving stations and people take their food to a table and find a seat. Speakers, attendees, volunteers, musicians, cooks, all sit together like one big family. Cutlery is in pots, wine is in carafes, water is in jugs, so there is a lot of pouring and passing and serving each other, which breaks the ice and kick-starts conversations.

The indoor dining spaces, like the food barn at Do Wales, are softly lit with twinkling lights and an abundance of candles. Greenery, like ferns and moss, dress the crevices in the old stone walls and window recesses. The table decorations are kept very simple: a single stem in an old milk bottle, a pebble or two holding paper napkins in place, a moss-covered log doubling up as a tea-light holder. The tables are old wooden trestle tables, and they are paired with a random mix of folding chairs, stools and benches. The dining experience spills out of the food barn to a court-yard covered by a bespoke canvas awning which has been made to hug a copper beech tree in the centre of the space and provides shelter from rain or shade from the sunshine.

The Do Garden

Directly outside the lecture barn we have a kitchen garden. There are eleven raised beds where we plant things that can be picked for the table or the vase. The garden by no means produces all the vegetables we eat, but we can step out of the kitchen and pick herbs and salad leaves as the mood takes us.

In the Do Garden, herbs stand side by side with sunflowers. Heady scented sweetpeas ramble up willow branches leaving mint and lemon balm swaying below. There are no formal rows of perfect vegetables here. The oxeye daisies, foxgloves and poppies ensure the lines are softened and the boundaries between order and chaos blurred. If you are lucky, you might find a strawberry hiding beneath a rhubarb leaf or a tomato ripening in the shelter of a kale leaf. If left long enough, you discover that the vegetables that have gone to seed often produce the prettiest of flowers.

The planting brief for the Do Vegetable Garden is simple: Optimum visual impact plus maximum yield for the first weekend in July. Between planting and harvest we are at the mercy of whatever the weather throws at us. We have planted peas that have perished under heavy winds, we have lost lettuces to greedy creatures, but somehow every year, the garden manages to put on a vibrant display of colourful flowers and striking seedheads, and the herbs and salads are enjoyed by all.

Decorating with flowers and foliage

The flowers we grow are not exotic or showy, they are simple, country flowers that look at home on a Welsh farm. Sweet peas, roses, cornflowers, poppies, oxeye daisies all ramble and self-seed through the gardens. They are picked and placed in miniature vases as single blooms for windowsills or grouped in small bunches on the tables. A simple display in a glass vessel is elevated when placed in front of the vibrant green of a moss-stained wall.

For a large part of the year, our climate is mild and damp, so we have plenty of green foliage, lichen covered branches and lush ferns to pick and use. We add them to crevices in the cool, stone walls of the barns and they seem to bring a calm, peaceful atmosphere to the spaces.

The Do stylists' toolbox

1. Pebeo 4Artist Markers 4mm in white. Oil-based opaque, glossy makers that can be used on wood, metal, plastic, glass, ceramics and much more.

2. A staple gun.

3. A hot glue gun.

4. Refillable gas lighters to light candles.

5. Twine.

6. Florist's wire.

7. Plastic watering tubes and caps, for hydrating single stems of foliage or flowers in displays.

8. A selection of nails, screws, hooks and tacks.

9. Chalk pens of various nib sizes.

10. Heavy-duty sticky tape.

Do signage

One of the daily duties at the Do Lectures is updating the chalkboards. We have chalkboards for workshops, for the daily menu and for the talks' schedule. We put a lot of effort into writing these boards; the style of the lettering, the use of quirky illustrations, the choice of words – they are all extensions of the way we look after and communicate to our attendees. They are an informal way of keeping everyone up-to-date with what's happening, allowing us to communicate in our own Do style.

Taking our time to create a thing of beauty that could easily disappear in the rain and is going to be wiped away and replaced a few hours after its creation, is worth all the effort. For us it's about making every little detail reflect who we are, no matter how short-lived it might be.

We don't just chalk on chalkboards. We use pieces of slate, stone and pebbles to communicate simple information. Chalk is also a great way to present the best quotes from the talks: almost as soon as the words have been spoken, they appear in hidden places as a reminder of the day's events.

At some of the past Do Lectures we have been joined by artists who have turned inspirational words from the talks into pieces of art. At Do USA, Cumbersome Multiples set up a printing press in the back of the Hop Barn and printed posters of the words spoken by the speakers as they were doing their talks. At Do Wales, paper-cut artist Erica Francis George made stencils during the talks and sprayed the words in hidden spots around the farm to the delight of those that found them.

LU

AFT

Thursday Me[nu]

[LUN]CH

herby pea broth [VEGAN]
local bread
Caws Cenarth pearl
wen cheese

[AFTE]RNOON

Bapa birth
[le]mon + date bars
[wi]th chocolate

SUPPER

A...
D...
Ra...
On...
rhu...
pear...
gar...

PUDDING

f...

How to build a campfire

If you were to describe the Do Lectures as a smell, it would be woodsmoke. While the attendees are still sleeping, our dawn shift volunteers are busy lighting the many fires that are dotted around the farm. Nothing is more welcome for a bleary-eyed camper than a warm fire and a hot cup of tea. Throughout the day the fires become meeting points; a chance to chat and make a new friend. The wheelbarrow is constantly trundled back and forth to the woodpile and it feels like there is always someone strolling past with an armful of logs. At the end of the night the fires make good stopping points to have one last drink before heading off to bed.

When we source the wood for our fires, we don't just consider how the wood burns, but we also think about how it smells. We look for a variety of wood: Small-cut quick-burning logs to get the fire going; larger denser logs to sustain the fire and increase the heat, and fragrant-smelling orchard woods to enhance the smell.

Our perfect combination of fire wood is:

Birch to get the fire going. It's a great burning wood with good heat.
It burns fast so is an ideal fire-starter. Once the fire is established, some
good woods to add next are ash, oak or blackthorn. Ash is one of the best
woods to burn, it gives good heat, produces a flame and it burns nice and
slowly. Similarly, oak gives a good lasting heat and burns reasonably slow.
Blackthorn is another slow burner and has the advantage of not being too
smoky. We then add an orchard wood like apple or pear; they both burn
well but better still, they give off a fragrant smell as they burn.

Most of our fires are built in fire bowls. We inherited a small collection
of cast iron coppers when we moved to the farm, plus we have collected
a few more from salvage yards and farm sales over the years. Apparently
they were used to boil large amounts of water for the household to use. But
we have also heard stories of them being used to cook feed for animals.
Now, they have a new life as fire bowls. They enable us to make deep,
warm and contained fires. Fires that are easy to start and to keep going.
And of course, they look completely at home on the farm.

Showering Do style

Unlike most camping experiences, taking a shower at the Do Lectures is a truly pleasurable experience. There are two different shower areas, one in an old stone barn and the other in a purpose-built tin-clad building. From the outside both buildings look like typical agricultural buildings. Inside, the shower enclosures have been built using tin sheet, reclaimed wood and concrete. The beauty of the showers is that they offer total privacy but are open to the roof rafters, so when you shower, you look up into the eaves of the building and they give you a sense of being outdoors even though you are sheltered. Better still, the showers at Do USA in Campovida are not contained within a building (the benefit of reliable weather), so when you look up, you are seeing a starry sky.

The steam from the rainhead showers releases the wonderful aroma of mint and lemon balm as it mingles with generous bunches of herbs tied to the showerheads. There's a continuous supply of clean fluffy towels, so you don't need to keep a damp towel in your tent. And when you go to the sink area to brush your teeth, you are rewarded with a view of the River Teifi meeting the sea.

Staying warm and cosy

There's a price to pay for our lush green landscape and coastal views: unpredictable weather. One minute we might be enjoying a gentle breeze on a warm sunny afternoon and the next we might be seeking shelter from lashing rain and howling wind. The benefit of being on a hillside overlooking the bay is that we get to watch the weather roll in from the sea, so we do get some warning that we need to take cover under one of our bespoke canvas awnings.

As well as the campfires that constantly burn, we make sure we have some cosy corners with a pile of Welsh blankets and warm sheepskins to snuggle into. Our soft wool blankets are made by Melin Tregwynt, a mill not far from Cardigan that has been run by the same family for three generations.

When it's time for bed, attendees can help themselves to a hotwater bottle to take back to their tent from the 'pamper' station in the field. Here they will also find everything they need to make a hot drink should they wake up early and want to take a cup of something back to bed to listen to the dawn chorus.

'Carefully, beautifully designed to create
the conditions for magic to happen.
Go and you'll know what I mean'
Past attendee

'The uncomfortable process
of completely removing
yourself from your normal
life and your comfortable
sofa and addictive HBO
series is exactly what makes
the Do Lectures a good idea'.

Past attendee

Discomfort

There is also an element of discomfort at the Do Lectures. This is one of the things that sets it apart from most other events, which are often held in soulless conference centres and characterless hotels.

The environment is open to the elements, and the weather in west Wales is changeable. Meals are often eaten under canvas shelters. Straw bales and tree stumps replace sofas and armchairs. At one of the early Do Lectures, it rained heavily from start to finish and there was a genuine need to huddle around the campfires and drink copious amounts of hot tea just to keep warm. It was hard going, but at the end everyone had a genuine sense of self-pride and embraced the fact that they were more resilient than they thought.

Sleeping under canvas and sharing a tent with people you've never met before can also be a challenge (we do now give people the option to pay a little extra for a tent of their own) but it's often these situations that create the best experiences.

Your 'roommates' become the people you sit with at breakfast, the ones you look out for as you leave the cowshed, and the ones you might share thoughts on the day with late into the night. Quite often, the few days spent in a tent together, lead to great friendships that last long after the event.

When you return home to your familiar surroundings and comfortable bed, the smell of wood smoke in your hair and the mud on your shoes are your badges of honour – reminders that you can step out of your comfort zone and still feel completely at home.

Do After Dark

As the sun goes down on a day at the Do Lectures, it's time to sit by a campfire and listen to some music. The outdoor stage, situated in the heart of the farm, becomes the focal point for all the action in the hours of darkness. A whole load of thought and attention goes into planning the Do After Dark schedule.

Something soothing and mellow is a good idea for the first night, or perhaps a poet or comedian to lighten the mood and bring the audience together through laughter.

On day two, a Welsh male voice choir, singing their hearts out in their mother tongue, has been known to provoke a tear or two, and this has been followed by even more raw emotion from Do favourite, singer/songwriter Luke Sital-Singh, who sings of love, loss and sadness while the audience listen on from old Persian rugs and hay bales scattered beneath a starry sky.

On the last night, the mood switches to party. The talks are done, everyone is physically tired and emotionally drained, and dancing is what is required. A live band kickstarts the action and gets everyone moving. Some of the best bands have got everyone on their feet, performing encore after encore, their set exhausted, the band just jamming along to the mood of the audience. Once the dancing starts, it has to carry on, so the evening usually ends with a silent disco.

The silent disco started at Do USA as a way to protect the neighbours from sound pollution – the geography of Campovida means sound travels for miles. What started as a problem needing to be solved quickly became a magical Do After Dark moment. The wireless headphones have a range of up to 100m and the party spread out through Campovida's stunning gardens – all that could be seen dotted around were the lights flashing on the headphones like fireflies in the night sky. The silent disco then made an appearance at Teen Do in Wales. It was a perfect way to get everyone dancing, as the different channels meant the teens could listen to one playlist and the adults another. The silent disco is now a firm Do ritual, a good way to keep dancing into the early hours without disturbing those who have made their way to bed … and we're sure the neighbours are grateful too.

James Morton, Do Wales 2017

Kizzy Crawford, Do Wales 2015

Luke Sital-Singh, Do Wales 2015

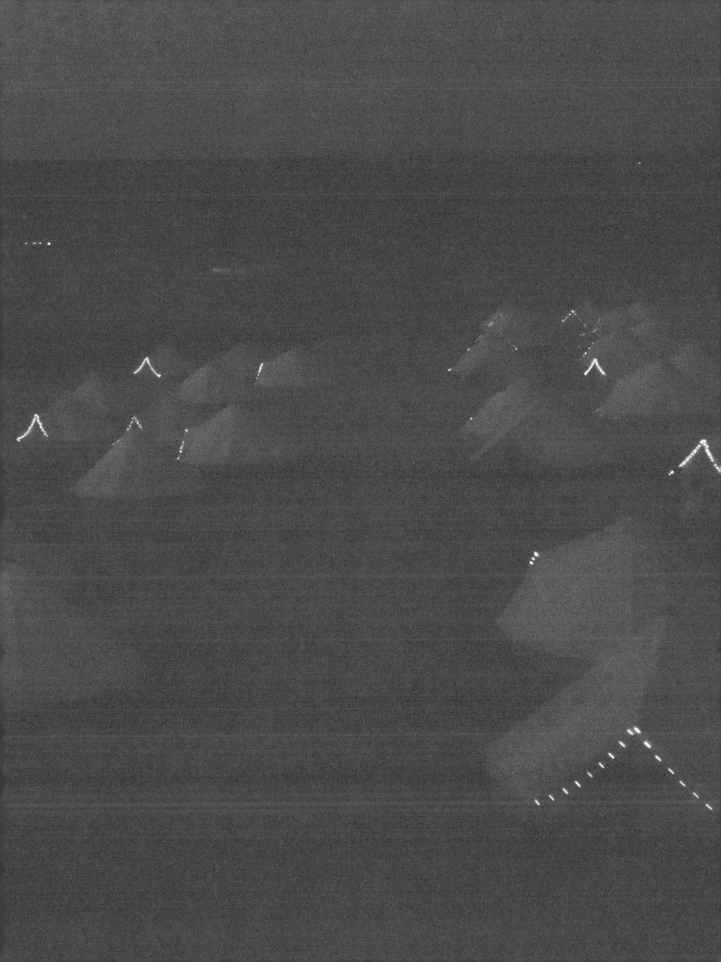

The intangible things

Not every detail is a physical thing that you can see and touch. It's often the little things that impact the way you feel that can have the biggest effect. And often this is down to the people. At Do we are lucky to have the support of a great team of people from our small in-house team, our founding partners and our community of volunteers and supporters who help us in so many ways.

The spirit of Do is one of giving and sharing, summed up by our mantra 'Givers get lucky.' The best people we have worked with are the ones that will do anything to help anyone, the caring ones, the smilers. There's no better way to feel part of a community, than to be welcomed in with open-armed warmth and love.

10 ways to Do the details

1. Consider everything. Every tiny detail.

2. Don't strive for perfection. Crumbling plaster, peeling paint and lichen covered stone can make beautiful backdrops for a vase of flowers or flickering candle.

3. Look at your space as if you are a guest who has just arrived. What do you see, smell, feel first?

4. Leave secret things for people to discover: a message behind a door; a candle in a gap in a stone wall; a pebble on a window ledge. Small things that most people won't even notice. But even if they bring pleasure to just one or two people, they are worth doing.

5. Source materials, flowers and foliage from the locality.

6. Create small, quiet spaces where people can take themselves away from the crowd – not everyone is an extrovert.

7. Keep fires burning and candles flickering. Buy more candles than you think you will need and invest in eight-hour tea lights and gas lighters.

8. Let the natural beauty of your space be the hero and make sure the things you add enhance it, not overpower it.

9. Add words. Informal signs with well-chosen words, a hand-written baggage tag or welcome note, hidden messages chalked or stenciled in unexpected places, big, bold phrases to welcome people in. They all add to the magic.

10. Don't be too precious or serious. Add touches that make people smile.

Ripples
and Community

'Amazing to share stories and experiences with people that 'get you'. One of the first times I've ever been surrounded by people that are similarly quietly ambitious, dedicated, driven and have the ability to think big. So many people think so small it can be crippling.'

Past attendee

The Do Lectures started as a small weekend event in Wales for just 40 people. Over 10 years it has evolved and grown. There have been Do Lectures events in America and Australia. There are over 350 talks online providing free education and inspiration for the thousands of people who visit the website. It hosts regular workshops to help people in business and life. It has inspired the creation of the Do Book Company that publishes useful and practical books by individuals who have spoken at Do. But perhaps the biggest success of the Do Lectures is the community that has built up around it.

The community is something the Do Lectures has no control over. It is created by a discussion over dinner between two strangers meeting for the first time. It starts with a compelling call to arms from a speaker as they finish their speech. It is fuelled by late-night promises in the gin bar as a group of people put the world to rights. Some great things have happened because of Do.

Trust

The Do Lectures has evolved in the way it has because of one simple thing: Trust. Take, for example, the story of how Do USA happened. Duke Stump was a speaker at Do Wales 2009. He tells the story of how he got upgraded on his flight over to London and so he made best use of the bar and landed feeling a little worse for wear. He then slept for the whole five-hour car journey from London to Wales. When he woke up he was in the middle of nowhere 'in the forest' in a place that just blew his mind. He loved being at Do, and we loved having him. His enthusiasm and passion brought such a positive energy to the event – and we connected with him from the start.

Just before he came to Do Wales, he had visited his friends Anna Beuselinck and Gary Breen at their new property, an old winery in Northern California. It struck him that it would make a good home for an American version of the Do Lectures. He put the idea to us, and I think David said something along the lines of, 'Great, tell us when it is and we'll put the Do sign in the post'. Duke thought we were joking and that we would obviously come up with long list of terms and conditions along with extensive guidelines on the do's and don'ts of putting on a Do Lectures event, but we didn't. Do USA was formed on a simple handshake based on the feeling that we could trust our baby in Duke's hands.

And our instinct was right. There have been five great Do USA events and whenever we have visited, we have returned inspired, refreshed and excited to bring some of their way of doing things into our way of doing things.

I'm a firm believer that people should listen to their heart and gut more, to put trust in their instincts. And when that is combined with trust in other people, amazing things can happen.

This belief was reinforced and summed up beautifully by Tina Roth Eisenberg during her talk at Do USA in 2013. 'Trust breeds magic', she said. I couldn't have put it better myself.

Watch Duke's talk: thedolectures.com

'There's something about being away from the rest of the world that gives you moments of perspective.'

Past attendee

Ripples:

Maggie Doyne
*Mother of 50 Nepalese children
and founder of the BlinkNow Foundation.*

Maggie Doyne, the 23-year-old American who had started an orphanage and was building a school in Nepal, was a speaker at Do Wales in 2010. She had been introduced to us via Duke Stump and Anna Beuselinck from Do USA.

Maggie's story has been woven into the fabric of the Do Lectures in many ways and through many people. Her talk moved the audience so much, that people felt compelled to support her and money was raised through our auction to support her children. Anna Felton, a former clothing designer, who worked for the Do Lectures, ended up going to Nepal to help Maggie set up a women's centre where they created a sustainable business making clothing.

In 2012, Anjali Karki, one of Maggie's adopted children, travelled with Maggie to Do Lectures USA to tell her story. Anjali's talk moved fellow speaker Cheryl Strayed so deeply that she and Maggie became firm friends. At the same time Maggie also met Libby DeLana (one of Do Lectures USA's core volunteers) and Libby now sits on the board of BlinkNow, Maggie's organisation. Two years later Maggie returned to Do Lectures USA as a participant, and during that time danced with a friend of Libby's, Jeremy Power Regimbal. That dance led to a loving marriage and, earlier this year, the birth of a beautiful baby girl, Ruby Sunshine.

Watch Maggie's talk: thedolectures.com

Matthew Helt
and **Do Lectures USA**

Matthew Helt was the first ever applicant of Do Lectures USA. He sold his bike to raise the funds to attend the 2011 event and was so inspired by his experience that he penned a letter in his teepee and left it for all future participants, telling them what to expect.

His letter acted as reinforcement for the Do USA team to carry on and commit to a second event. It also became a guide for the team on how to improve for the following year. Matt returned as a volunteer and helped produce the event. He introduced the team to some of their most memorable speakers, including Tina Roth Eisenberg and Daniel Epstein.

After speaking, Daniel Epstein ended up returning to Campovida on a mission to help bring an end to young girls' poverty through his Unreasonable events. That's when he met Alice and Ross Beese. Alice and Ross are from Wales and Alice's father, Andy Middleton, is one of the founding partners of the Do Lectures. Andy had encouraged his daughter and son-in-law to volunteer at Do Lectures USA. Alice and Ross went on to travel the world working with Daniel and the Unreasonable team.

When you speak with Matt today, he openly gives credit to the Do Lectures for transforming his life. Little did he know that selling his bike, would end up transforming the lives of others too.

Miranda West

Founder and publisher of The Do Book Company

Miranda got in touch to ask if we had considered publishing books by some of our speakers. She hadn't attended the Do Lectures at that point but earlier that day she had watched one of the talks online, 'Considering the Future of Books' by Craig Mod. This led her to discover the website and find out more about the Do Lectures before sending a speculative email to the info@ address. We Skyped, learnt that Miranda had a background in book publishing, talked about what a book company might look like, and invited her to attend the next event. The idea was to publish a curated series of books by Do Lectures speakers to allow anyone interested to delve deeper into a topic and to provide a stepping stone from the talk to actually doing.

Miranda set up the Do Book Company and launched in 2013 with five books. The covers are designed by James Victore, himself a Do Lectures speaker. The books are beautifully designed paperbacks that focus on the 'doing' not the background theory. New books are added each year and the company now has distribution around the world. The Do Lectures receives a royalty share from copies sold and this helps to sustain the event. It also helps us to spread the word – now some people are finding out about the Do Lectures through the books. Miranda comes to the event each year to listen to all the talks and come up with ideas for new books. In 2015 we got her to talk about her startup journey.

Watch Miranda's talk: thedolectures.com

'Staying within your comfort zone
won't help you think differently.'
Past attendee

Matt Lane
Founder of Beerbods, attended Do Wales 2012

Beerbods is a craft beer tasting club. Subscribers get sent a case every 12 weeks containing 12 beers. Every week they get emailed information about one of the beers and the idea is that on a Thursday evening everyone drinks the same beer and joins in the online live tasting.

Matt's Do Lectures journey started with him watching the online talks, led to him launching his company while he was at Do Wales 2012, and later saw him return as a speaker in 2015. He even recruited 'employee number 2' through the Do Lectures network. In his talk, Matt told the story about how on the Friday night of Do Wales, he was feeling all 'powered up' and ready to quit his day job (Beerbods was just a side project at this time). On the Saturday he managed to get an internet connection and he launched a holding page on his website introducing his business. Later that day he started talking to people about Beerbods as if it already existed. Someone tweeted about it and it was also featured on a live podcast from the event. By the time he got home 250 people had signed up and his business was launched.

'Another thing happened whilst I was there. A grenade went off in my head. The plan I had been working on wasn't finished but I needed to start this project now. So I started telling people my idea as if it already existed. Then weirdly, it did exist. I registered it as a business the day after I got home.'

Watch Matt's talk: thedolectures.com

Tom Fishburne
Founder of Marketoonist
attended the first Do Lectures in 2008

Tom Fishburne attended the Do Lectures in 2008 and returned as a speaker in 2011. He credits, or you could even say he blames, the Do Lectures for 'pushing him in the direction he wanted to go' and quit his job in business to become a cartoonist.

As a kid, Tom had wanted to become a cartoonist, but he took the sensible route and went to Harvard Buisness School and entered the world of business and marketing. He attended his first Do Lectures' event as a marketing director of Method and, when he returned to do his talk three years later, it was to tell the story of how he did eventually become a cartoonist.

Tom attended his first Do Lectures wondering what his story would be, were he ever to do a talk. The answer came to him while he was at the event. He voiced it at the Do Lectures and when he returned home he couldn't shake it. He eventually took the plunge, despite having the responsibility of a large mortgage and young family. He left his job and set himself up as a cartoonist. He even entitled his 2011 Do Lecture's talk 'Be careful what you wish for in this tent' as a way to highlight the impact the Do Lectures can have on you.

Tom's company is called Marketoonist and is founded on the belief that cartoons can help businesses communicate, and that businesses that communicate better are better businesses.

'The Do Lectures is the one event I've attended that I can honestly say left me changed. A lot of events claim that, but when I first attended the Do Lectures ... I left with a changed worldview that manifested itself in changing my life.'

Watch Tom's talk: thedolectures.com

'Hard to put into words but it is the single most influential event in my life so far. It has given me some form of moral code which I now try to live by. And meeting everyone there gave me the confidence to know I am not the only one with those views.'

Past attendee

Do workshops

We think of the Do Lectures as an encouragement network. A community that helps you be your best self. The annual three-day events aren't the only way people participate in the community. Ten years of talks are online for people to access for free wherever they are in the world and whenever they want to watch them. The Do Book Company is a thriving publishing house that has published 20 (and counting) books written by past speakers to help people learn a new skill or improve their life or business.

There are also regular one-day workshops hosted by past speakers or members of the Do community that offer subject-specific mini Do experiences exploring a topic in more depth than is possible in a 20 minute talk. It could be growing a business, learning presentation skills, communicating your personal story or making jam. These are held year-round at the Do Farm in Wales, in London, in New York and in California. The workshops keep the dialogue flowing, the inspiration hitting and the community alive.

'Since getting home connections are already being made. I have introduced people and been put in touch with others who are able to help, support or share, allowing us to take steps forward in our individual (collective) missions to do good and have fun doing it.'

Past attendee

Myths
and
Legends

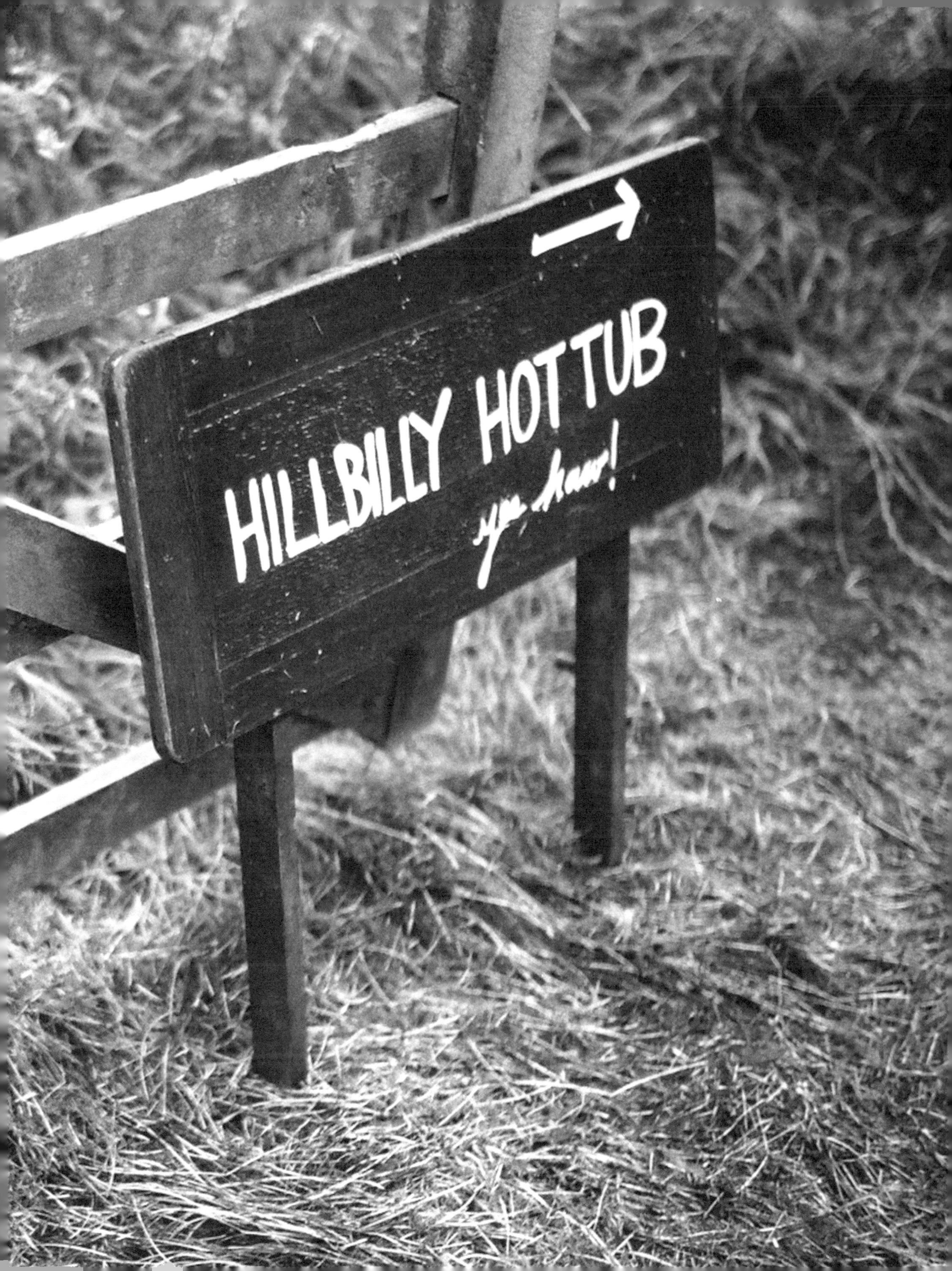
HILLBILLY HOT TUB
yee haw!

Do is all about creating an environment where 'magic' can happen. This is the unknown, but most exciting, bit of the event. All we do is create a space, invite the speakers and select the attendees, the rest is up to chance, the alignment of the stars and who you happen to sit next to at dinner.

Secret spaces, cosy nooks, little hideaways with open fires. A few hay bales and Welsh blankets in a quiet corner. Candlelight and wood smoke. Talks that open your mind. Music that stirs your soul. Magic isn't contrived. It can't be faked. It just needs an open door and a warm welcome to come on in and do its stuff.

Alastair Humphreys, the micro-adventurer, arrived a little late for his talk in 2009. He explained that he had stopped on the way and taken a dip in our local river, the Teifi. 'If you see a river, jump in it' fast became a motto for the event and spurred lots of river jumps and swims in both the Teifi and the Russian River (near Do USA) in the years to come.

For Do Wales 2016, we created a secret gin bar. We didn't tell anyone of its existence, we just let it be discovered. Word soon got out. By the second night, we had drunk the bar dry and Tom Herbert, the baker, was passing a freshly baked loaf of sourdough head-height around the crowded bar, so everyone could take a piece and join in the ritual of breaking bread together.

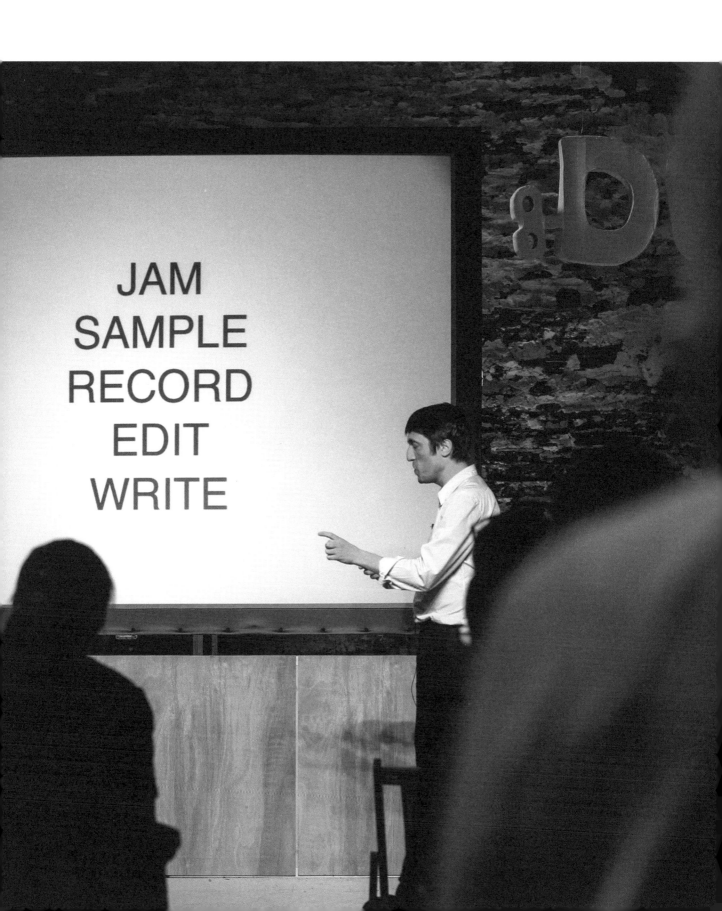

Radiohead's Colin Greenwood did a talk on the Sunday morning of Do Wales 2015. We kept it low key. We didn't film it. It was just a magical moment for the 100 people in the barn (and a big tick on the bucket-list for us).

Gabriel Branby, an axe maker and speaker at Do Wales 2009, brought a car boot full of axes with him so we could have some fun chopping wood. However, he was returning to Sweden by plane and he was concerned about taking his axes through customs, so he offered them up to be auctioned. This was the birth of the Do Auction, the fun fund-raising finale to the talks.

Mark Shayler gets ready to compere the Do Auction.

10 best moments of magic at Do

1. An impromptu wild swim in the River Teifi after Alastair Humphrey's call to action: 'If you see a river, jump in it.'

2. The passing of the loaf on the night the secret gin bar was discovered.

3. Dancing through the gardens during the silent disco at Campovida.

4. The choir workshop at Do Wales 2018 that led to a goose-bump inducing performance of a love song to the rest of us.

5. The first Do Auction, formed because there were a bunch of axes that the founder of Gränsfors Axes didn't want to take back through customs.

6. The surprise appearance of the giant puppet 'Bran' at Do Wales 2012.

7. Early-morning 'Rimming' (running and swimming) from the banks of the River Teifi to the sea.

8. The legendary saxophone player James Morton serenading the sunrise (for those that hadn't yet made it to bed) at Do Wales 2017.

9. Ken's shed at Campovida (apparently).

10. Volunteer swims at Mwnt beach after all the guests have left and everything has been put away.

Do Wales 2016:
Blaenporth Male Voice Choir sing
songs of love and longing in their
native tongue.

Will Parsons and Guy Hayward from the British Pilgrimage Trust walked the 70 miles from the source of the River Teifi to speak at Do Wales 2016. We joined them for the last few miles of their pilgrimage as they made their way to the mouth of the river at Poppit Sands.

The Hillbilly Hot Tub. Light a fire, wait a while, sit back and enjoy the view.

When the attendees and speakers have gone and the farm is spick and span, the volunteers and Do team go to Mwnt Beach for a celebratory swim.

Photographer Magdalena
Wosinska creating art at
Do Wales 2016.

End of
NORMAL

*Meeting attendees at the
train station, Do Wales 2017.*

Changing Times

The Do Lectures has evolved and changed to reflect what is happening in the world at the time. Looking back at the talks over the last 10 years, we've realised that we have gradually built up our own archive that does the same.

When we first started, the emphasis was very much on sustainability and the environment. A few years later, stories from the world of tech and entrepreneurship came to the fore. Food, health and wellbeing were soon to follow, and more recently, a new, more female-centred dialogue has begun to emerge.

The stories that are told at Do will always bear witness to what is happening in the world at large, and none of us can predict where the next decade will take us.

THE
STRESS
REPORT

⚡ Observation
and Enquiry

HUSTLE   HUSTLE

MELTDOWN

$20 US

£12 UK

THE
SIDE PROJECT
REPORT

+ Observation
and Enquiry

$20 US

Two reports produced by the
Do Lectures that delve deeper
into themes that have been
touched on in some of the talks.

2008 – 2018: Going up

Vegan meals

Dairy alternatives

Flat whites

Female attendees

Female speakers

Wild swimming

Instagram posts

Electric car charging points

Massage appointments

Alcohol-free cocktails

Campfire singing

Themes 2008

Ambition

Work

Big adventure

Following your path

Changing the world

Telling your story

Trusting your instinct

Big thinking

Inventing

Male

Themes 2018

Contentment

Time

Simple pleasures

Going with the flow

Changing yourself

Listening to others

Trusting the universe

Big feeling

Re-learning

Female

A Journey Worth Making

by Dr. Hugh Griffiths

To visit the Do Lectures once is a remarkable experience but to be invited to come back over several years to help understand its impact was an adventure. That was the challenge of my 'Do' when I was commissioned to study the event by David and Clare Hieatt through a research partnership with Cardiff University and the Welsh Government. My job was to be curious and 'stay curious', exploring the whats and whys of the influence of this event on those who participated or watched the talks online.

One year, the Do Lectures had a letterpress postcard made with the words 'Ideas Change Things', and they certainly do. However, I found that the ideas that changed things the most were not necessarily the many amazing ideas presented through the talks. Instead it was the courage and originality of the Do Lectures event format, whether held in Cardigan, California or beyond. As Paul Kaan, a digital strategist and wine maker, wrote when he visited Wales, the Do Lectures is 'carefully, beautifully designed to create the conditions for the magic to happen. Go and you'll know what I mean.' Perhaps it is surprising, particularly when you appreciate the quality of the speakers and their ideas, that the most significant essence of the event is not to be found in the content but the context. One participant expressed it rather wryly: 'The Do Lectures. It's not about the lectures.'

The quality of the talks is essential but it is the wider event experience that has proved to be the most critical factor in making the Do Lectures both memorable and transformative for so many of those who attend. The impact is in the medium, as well as in the message.

Without doubt the details of the event design are highly effective in stimulating personal change and challenging those who participate. The social dynamics, setting and structure of the event does much more than provide a nudge towards achieving a little more or making some minor, incremental adjustment in their lives. For many, it creates a fundamental personal push and generates both the inspiration and courage necessary to make radical shifts, and sometimes complete transformations, in their personal life and work. Projects with a clear social purpose have been born, innovative companies founded, business ideas given life, and purposeful career changes have all taken place at or through the Do Lectures. The event has created so much more than a platform for the amazing diversity of speakers that participate – the Do Lectures has created a theatre of change. Most apparent at the live events, but also online, the discourse of change is continually broadcast and reinforced, creating an inner conversation that allows for a complete reimagination of you, of your work and even of wider society. After experiencing the Do Lectures, many find that it provides a valuable new lens for looking at life and opportunity.

One of the significant factors that helps to create that impact are the 'micro-challenges' of being part of the event. The Do Lectures is not held in a comfortable hotel or easy-access conference centre; instead it is held on the Hieatts' farm on the west coast of rural Wales. Particularly if you are travelling internationally, just getting to this relatively remote location can be a challenge, and for most it is a completely unfamiliar environment. You arrive to the emotionally disruptive intensity of being among a crowd of strangers, sharing the relative discomfort of sleeping in a field under canvas, gathering for the lectures in a sometimes chilly barn building and spending most of the long weekend almost permanently outdoors. However, this is warmed by much conversation and shared meals together set in the beauty and sensory stimulation of the Welsh coastal landscape. It is a 'journey worth making' and in those few days and through the intensity of the social experience, a community forms – that gathering of strangers rapidly becomes a company of friends who often remain connected by all the opportunities of social and digital media.

Of course, the short lectures are themselves remarkable, and others in this book have already highlighted some of the 'talks that changed me'. Speakers such as Maggie Doyne, Mickey Smith, Sean Carasso and James Alexander are undoubtedly influential, but these stand-out talks are just four from several hundred presented from the Do Lectures stage and then made available online for free. When asked which of the talks had influenced them the most, people tended to say, 'It's hard to pick out individual talks against the experience of being there,' or something similar. But when pressed, those who responded recalled a very broad cross-section of lectures, sometimes in great detail, sometimes several years after being at the event, which tells you something of the personal impact of attending. I am certainly not aware of another event where such a high proportion of talks are so well received and so well remembered by those who attend.

The coherency between the themes and ideas presented by the speakers and the design of the event itself is directly observable. For example, consider that speakers who are environmentalists, sustainability specialists and ecologists deliver their talks in an outdoor, rural setting; the adventurers, explorers and extreme sports enthusiasts speak to an audience who are camping outdoors at a relatively inaccessible location on the coast of Wales; founders of community-orientated projects or social innovators share stories of their work in an intensely social setting where high levels of personal interaction are purposefully included; disruptive ideas of innovation and entrepreneurship are presented in a setting that greatly contrasts with most people's everyday experience and routine; accounts of the professional and personal journeys of designers, photographers and artists are presented in a highly stylised environment surrounded by the drama and aesthetic pleasure of a rural landscape; Welsh entrepreneurs, musicians, politicians and other cultural partici- pants are given a profile on an international platform in a local place, Cardigan, with historical significance as the birthplace of the Eistedfodd instituted by the 12th-century Welsh prince Rhys ap Gruffydd. In this way, the themes and categories of the speakers are directly reflected to some degree in the real-world context of the event, establishing a meaningful connection between form and content.

Aside from its personal impact on those who attend, the Do Lectures has demonstrated that the lecture is certainly not dead. But it is clear that it needs substantial renegotiation in an age where we can access high-quality online content almost anywhere and at any time through our smartphones and other digital devices. Chris Anderson, president and curator of the TED talks, has described this new vitality given to the public lecture as something of a 'talk renaissance'. My research has demonstrated an important conclusion in that much of this renewal comes from the dynamics of the format rather than from the content being delivered. Great public speaking can deliver powerful words and ideas, but what is important is not just the presentation of knowledge – after all, this can be shared in so many other ways. Instead, one of the most significant things about the live lecture is its identity as a shared event and experience. It brings together the speakers and the listeners in a single location and for an irreproduceable moment, and in doing so creates a community of attention. The writer Ursula Le Guin described this bond as: 'Teller and listener, each fulfils the other's expectations. The living tongue that tells the word, the living ear that hears it, bind and bond us in the communication we long for.'

It is this bond that is so evident in the Do Lectures, a bond strengthened by the highly social design of the event that so effectively blurs the
boundaries between speakers and guests, platform and audience, lecture
programme and the meal-table. Tom Eldridge wrote about his experience
attending the Do Lectures in 2014 and expressed this very clearly:

'When I think of a lecture, a passenger of information comes to mind.
Questions can be asked but there is distance between the speaker and
the audience. The Do Lectures takes the opposite approach. There is no
distance. You break bread, you drink and you talk.'

Over the last few years I have spent many hundreds of hours collecting
and analysing data, speaking to attendees and investigating the detail
and context of this event and it is clear that David and Clare have created
something unique and original. There is certainly a legacy in the many
people it has inspired toward positive and fundamental change because
of attending the Do Lectures. Perhaps the lesson that will stay with me
the longest is not any single transformational idea, or personal story

shared from the platform, but that there is tremendous power in creating gatherings, places where personal connections can be made. The uncommon nature of the Do Lectures experience allows people to forge new relationships or professional links and the relaxed, egalitarian and highly personal atmosphere of the event encourages the formation of valued friendships and partnerships. These are not the relatively superficial or pragmatic links that develop from the more usual networking for business; they are much more meaningful and significant connections with others, their ideas and their inspirations. These are formed because of the deeply shared experience of the event and also because we see that other 'like-minded but highly individual people' are grappling with similar questions of life and purpose.

These questions are often difficult to consider in the routine of our everyday lives but they are essential if we are to make one of the most significant connections we need to find – the connection with ourselves and our identity. The Do Lectures challenge us to discover or uncover the meaning we can find in our everyday, encouraging us to actively choose how we spend our lives and to apply our time, energy and attention with purpose. As one attendee described it, the Do Lectures 'can give you the courage to win your life'.

A major portion of my research was focused on understanding the communications strategy as well as the experience of the Do Lectures. There are certainly many wider lessons from the Do Lectures that other forward-thinking organisations could reflect on in respect of their own brand communications and digital media. For example, the Do Lectures use of starkly contrasting high-tech and high-touch media forms has created an effective dynamic that is ideally suited to the present opportunities in technology and culture. They have established a high-contrast media ecology that provides a rich media texture and variation of experience for their audience, something that has significantly strengthened their ability to communicate. As a case study in strategic communications, the Do Lectures provide a compelling example for brands and organisations who want to achieve deeper, lasting and more authentic engagement with their audiences.

#dolectures

Afterword

From 28 June to 1 July 2018 we held our tenth Do Lectures event in Wales. It wasn't an easy time for us as a family. We had lost my father a few months before, our girls were in the middle of important school exams, plus we were in the process of moving our other business, Hiut Denim, into bigger premises. The tenth Do Lectures provided a pause in all our madness. The sun shone (it was in the middle of a very rare Welsh heatwave), the speakers delivered some of the most moving talks we have ever witnessed, and we were serenaded by an impromptu Do choir that sang the sweetest song about love. It was probably as perfect as we could have ever hoped it would be. It felt like it was a real celebration of a decade of Do.

Over ten years we have heard talks from over 350 speakers; their talks have been viewed online by over a million people. The last two events have been live-streamed so that the barn has been able to 'open its doors' to a bigger audience.

During these 10 years we have heard many a story about how the Do Lectures has changed people's lives. These stories are not flippant statements but genuine expressions of heartfelt appreciation. Every time we hear these tales we feel humbled. Events like the Do Lectures are important. People are looking for ways to connect with people who feel the same as them and care about the things they care about. They are searching for ways to re-set their path and find the courage to follow their dreams.

The Do Lectures is a beautiful thing. That's because it is a 'pure' event, created with the best intentions, untouched by commercialism and unrealistic growth targets (the barn can't get any bigger). The ticket sales and workshop proceeds keep a small team employed for the year and provide anyone in the world with access to a frcc educational platform. That's how we like it, and that's how we want it to stay.

Our challenge for the next decade is how to keep the beauty of being small, but enable the Do Lectures to benefit more people through events like one-day workshops and Teen Do, through live-streaming and by growing the online community.

Another exciting diversion for us is the potential of stand-alone companies forming on the back of the Do Lectures. Like-minded companies created to encourage and inspire people and to help them be their best selves. One great example of this is the Do Book Company. It was given a head start by being connected to the Do network, but it soon grew and, in turn, it brought back more people to the community. More and more, we are finding that people are getting to know about the Do Lectures because they have come across a Do Book. This is an exciting model that we are keen to explore. We believe that the community can grow through the formation of other companies or projects that follow the Do ethos and want to become part of an encouragement network. Who knows where this notion might lead, but it's a subject that's being discussed at our dinner table more and more frequently.

But back to now. And back to the barn on the Do Farm.

The Do Lectures event can't get any bigger. It will always be a small, intimate and beautiful gathering in the middle of nowhere, on the edge of Wales, or at the end of a highway in Northern California …

Speakers

Do Lectures Speakers
2008

John Grant

Alastair McIntosh

Andrew Whitley

Michael Fordham

Michael Braungart

Russell Davies

Matt Jones

Guy Watson

Ken Yeang

Gerald Cooper

Gavin Pretor-Pinney

Trevor Bayliss

Craftsmen, makers and artisan business founders.
Artists, photographers and graphic designers. Chefs and restauranteurs,
food growers and producers. Environmental, nature and outdoor
champions or adventurers. Local champions and place makers.
Digital platform entrepreneurs and technologists. A bunch of passionate
mavericks and change-makers. Challengers of thought. Provokers of debate.
Champions of change. Firestarters. Doers. Human beings.

Just like you. Just like me.

Yun Hider   Dafydd Davies   Cary Fowler

Timothy Ferris   Andy Cummins   Aubrey Meyer

Paul Chatterton   Tamsin Osmond   Andy Kirkpatrick

Speakers
2009

Duke Stump

Paul Deegan

Geoff McFetridge

Uffe Elbaeks

Tony Davidson

Jane Davidson

Patrick Holden

Gregor MacLennan

Alan Moore

Tom Taylor

Alice Taylor

Adam Lowry

Alastair Humphreys

Michael Pawlyn

Rolf Potts

Gerald Miles

Tim Birkhead

Gabriel Branby

Ben Hammersley

David Rosenberg

Andrew Reason

Speakers
2010

Brian John

David Spiegelhalter

Darina Allen

Alasdair Harris

Bill Drummond

Alex Haw

Craig Mod

Gerd Leonhard

James Lynch

Mark Earls

Euan Semple

Jay Rogers

Markus Brehler

Maggie Doyne

Paula Le Dieu

Steve Edge

Matt Webb

Peter Segger

Sir Tim Berners-Lee

Steve Glenn

Phil Parker

David Lloyd Owen

Alice Holden

David Allen

Ed Stafford

Daniel Seddiqui

Speakers 2011

Laura Miner

Alan Webber

Rob Poynton

Mickey Smith

Les McKeown

Perry Chen

Indy Johar

Colin Tudge

Michael Kelly

John Kearon

Mohammad Al-Ubaydli

Christiana Wyly

Rob Penn

Chido Govera

Arthur Potts Dawson

Frank Chimero

Neil Denny

Alistair Smith

Faisel Rahman

Tom Fishburne

Caroline Flint

Joe Casey

David & Alison Lea-Wilson

Glen Peters

Nick Hand

Zach Smith

Richard King

Mark Shayler

Speakers
2011 USA

Terry Kellogg

Nate Stanton

John Fetzen

Pam Weiss

Shira Lazar

Chris Henrikson

Jim Riswold

James Syhabout

Chris Allen

Cindy Meehl

David Hieatt

Adam Lamoreaux

The Buried Life

Ann Daniels

Sean Baker

Speakers
2012

Will Rosenzweig

Tim Drake

Tom Herbert

Sean Carasso

Mike Beeston

Sasha Dichter

Robin Sloan

Michael Acton Smith

Richard Askwith

Marion Deuchars

James Victore

Jane Ni Dhulchaointigh

James Bridle

Joel Bukiewicz

Gav Thompson

Brian Robertson

Edward Brown

Catherine Powell

Bobette Buster

Chris Heathcote

Andy Puddicombe

Wilson Miner

Anna Felton

Toshi Nakamura

Shan Williams

Marc Koska

Tim Smit

Speakers
2012 USA

Merely Benson-Rice

Orren Fox

James Freeman

Chief Arvol Looking Horse

Brenda Chapman

Cheryl Strayed

Charlie Engle

Anjali Karki

Cathy Bailey & Robin Petravic

Adam Stofsky

John Andreliunas

Allesandra Lariu

Speakers
2013

Matt Hart

Sam Pearce

Collyn Ahart

Owen Rogers

Scott Davis

Mark Boulton

Jonathan Rees

Adil Abrar

Tim Little

Andy Middleton

Damon Collins

Jenny Fielding

Min-Kyu Choi & Matt Judkins

Zach Klein

Alex Tutty

Paul Glover

Brandon Mendelson

Amy Jo Martin

Speakers
2013 USA

Jacques Panis

Brad Ludden

Wendy Palmer

Eduardo Garcia

Claire Herminjard

Tina Roth Eisenberg

Briony Penn

Daniel Epstein

Sean Scott

Steve Larosiliere

Anna Beuselinck & Gary Breen

Alice & Ross Beese

Guy Webster

Speakers
2014

Colin Greenwood

Evan Doll

Sarah Corbett

Lydia Winters

Rosa Park

Justin McMurray

Michael Townsend Williams

Hunter Lee Soik

Nick Gray

Fergal Smith

Lee Bolam

Rohan Anderson

Stef Lewandowski

Gavin Strange

Kasim Ali

Dr Sarah Beynon

Peter Saunders

Tom Farrand & Dan Burgess

Mo Syed

Stephanie Lynn

Irfon Watkins

Massoud Hassani

Carlo Navato

Nigel Annett

Roger Pride

Speakers
2014 Australia

Luke Pearson

Jan Stewart

Will Dayble

Louis-Jacques Darveau

Tim Ross

Shannon Eeles

Michelle Matthews

Hannah Cutts

Corinne Proske

Carly Heaton

Mark Reeves

Geoff Manchester

Peter Williams

Steve Killelea

Ross Hill

Tess & Graham Payne

Jeremy Forbes

Olivia Hilton

Nick Jaffe

Speakers
2014 USA

John Ash

James Alexander

Peter Farrelly

Rose Styron

Rich Hill

Adele Stafford

Maria Popova

Ben Masters

Elle Luna

Chipper Bro Bell

Colin Delehanty

Jodi Sagorin

Speakers
2015

Claire Elsdon

Ryan Holiday

Eamon Fullalove

Dan Rubin

Chris Barez Brown

Steve Evans

Steve Jennings

Dan Germain

James Wallman

David Marquet

Dan Kieran

Miranda West

Justin Drake

Anna Jones

David Punchard

CJ Bowry

Ciara Judge & Émer Hickey

Jack Adair Bevan

Tom Coleman

Matt Lane

Ben Edmonds

Ian Sanders

Neil McNair

Speakers
2015 USA

Anastasia Somoza

Ellen Bennett

Hall Newbegin

Kevin Pearce

Frank Escamilla

Katy Jeremko

Steve Wilson

Daryl Davis

Tyrone Poole

Speakers
2015 Australia

Dennis Mcintosh

Taylor Davidson

Annie Parker

Tamsin Carvan

Sandra Mahlberg

Kaitlin & Aaron Tait

Mat Lynn

Nicholas Gruen

Sarah Jane Pell

Rachael Beesley

Emilie Zoey Baker

John Elliott

Liz Leyshan

Andy Hedges

Marcus Veerman

Hamish Curry

Connie Johnson

Graeme Wise

Josh & Lauren Capelin

Speakers
2016

Meg Lobb

Michael Burne

Chris Sheldrake

Severine Von Tscharner Fleming

Gillian Davis

Konrad Brits

Heather LeFevre

Will Parsons & Guy Hayward

Kamal Mouzawak

Stephen Russell

Simon Wright

Anna Koska

Ian James & Nick Selby

Mr. Bingo

Rhys Newman

Daniela Papi Thornton

Matt Hackett

Ian Matthews

Robbie Hearn

John German

Holley Murchison

James Kerr

Robert McCrum

Magdalena Wosinska

Speakers
2016 USA

Winky Lewis

Roda Ahmed

Veronika Scott

Brandon 'BMIKE' Odums

Andrew Ference

Jedidiah Jenkins

Ally Maz

Brian Lindstrom

Jacqueline Sharp

John Finger

Mara Abrams

Miki Agrawal

Jerri Chou

Speakers
2017

Scott Colton

Jim Brunberg

Kate Berry

Kate Robinson

Adam Robinson

Rob Ryan

Brendan Tracey

Anna Young

Woody Tasch

Gregg Buchbinder

Ella Grace Denton

Floyd Woodrow

Dominic Wilcox

Sophie Thomas

Kym Pham

Charlie Gladstone

Rob Jones

Julien Millot

Alex Chung

Joshua Coombes

Nicky Spinks

Speakers
2018

Elle Luna

Amanda Blainey

Matt 'Mills' Miller

Alastair Humphrys

Vicki Saunders

Paul Sinton-Hewitt

Ben Branson

Katie Elliott

Giles Duley

Tina Roth-Eisenberg

Kristin Hallenga

Duke Stump

Andrew Paynter

Christy Mcfarlane

Geoff Mcfetridge

Bobette Buster

Romy Fraser

Dave Evans

Dearbhla Reynolds

Angelo Morgan-Somers

Alan Maskin

Glen Peters

James Sills

About the author

Clare Hieatt is the co-founder of the Do Lectures and Hiut Denim. She started her working life in London as a copywriter. She moved back to Wales with her husband, David, 18 years ago, and together they have been concentrating on building businesses with a purpose and raising their two daughters.

Thanks

The author and publisher are grateful to the following readers who pledged their support and helped to make this book happen:

Nuno Abreu
Elle Adams
Mel Adams
Mark Aink
Marcus Ainley
Paul Alderson
ALT-Architecture
Dave Andrews
Richard Arron
Jonny Baker
Christian Banfield
Sebastiaan Barbé
Miranda Bates
Algy Batten
Richard Beaven
Alex Bec
Becky
Alice Beese
Tracey Bellow
Steven Bennett-Day
Andrew Bennie
Anna Beuselinck
& Gary Breen
October Bishop
Kelly Black
Ethan Bodnar
Lee Bolam
Agatha Bolla
Mark Bottomley
Anna Bowen
Hillary Bowen
Tim Bowles
Martin Boyle
Lisa Brady
Carla Brewington
Jo Briggs
James Brittain
Fiona Brown
Sylvie Bryant
Stephen P. Buckley
Andrew Budgen
Toby Bull
Dan Burgess
Michael Burne
Diane Burridge
Bobette Buster

Abbi Buszard
Andi Butterworth
Matt Callanan
Cristina Camarena
Matthew Carle
Neal Chant
C.C. Chapman
Chapter
Chris Clark
Phil Clarke
Justine Clement
Jake Clifford
Keith M. Cochran
Adrian Cockle
Deborah Colella
Sarah Corbett
Denise Cornell
Mike Coulter
& Carol Coulter
Jane Craigie
Dauan, Johanne & Choi
Louisa Daubney
Ben Davies
Nia Davies
Mark Davison
Alistar Dean
Nathalie Delaney
Mr & Mrs Deli
Kirstie Drummond Papworth
Tom Eagar
Ruth Eastelow
Carlos Echegaray
Gareth Edwards
Kate Edwards
Louise Edwards
Simon Edwards
Ian Ellison
Ben Emmens
Sue Fan
Charles Fanshawe
Paul Farmiga
Catt Fields White
David Fletcher
Jan Fortune
Helen Francis
Rory Franklin

Stephen Furness
Mariken Gaanderse
Hilary Gallo
Aitor Garcia
Jan Garde
Darja Gartner
Mark Geljon
Emma Gibbs De Oliveira
James Gibson
Alastair Gill
Robert Glazier
Mark Goddard
Arturo Goicochea Hoefken
Nick Goring
Ben Govier
Grabbins
Kathryn Grace
J D Grant
Great Dane Coffee
Hugh Griffiths
Stu Grimshaw
Jo Guest
Lauren Guida
Muhz Ham
Stuart Hardman
Tom Harfleet
Gareth Harris
Matt Harrison
Dominic Hartley
Scott Hawthorn
Perry Haydn Taylor
Olly Headey
Stephen Heath
Cornel Hess
Paul Hindmarsh
Ruth Huddleston
Will Hudson
David Hughes
Jason Hunt
Jamie Huskisson
Hywel
Phill James
Rory Jeffers
Chester Jenkins
Mike Jenkins
Kenji Jesse

Gareth Jones
Simon Jones
Matthew Judkins
Birgit Käsbeck
Gareth Kay
Rebecca Kaye
Beth Kempton
Matt Keogh
Ben Kerr
Jon Khoo
Dan Kieran
Stephen King
Lue Kraltchev
Ian Laird
Julie Laming
Matthew Lammas
Anna Lamotte
Diane Law
James Leitch
Tim LeRoy
Sara Lewis
Simon Lilly
John Limb
Fiona Lindsell
Lost In The Forest Institute
Ross MacDonald
Peter Mance
Francesca Marchegiano
Christopher Margenout
Claire Margetts
Diane McCrea
Mark McCullough
Ciara McGarrity
Graeme McGowan
Kim McGowan
Shaughn (Shamus) McGurk
Bob McInnis
Zephyr Mercer
Krasina Mileva
Nick Miller
Catherine Mooney
Jeanette Mooney
Samantha Morgan
Lorna Morris
Steve Murray
All the team at Nest.co.uk
Andrea Norrington
Uzo Okwuosa
Andrea Oleniczak
Jo Oliver
Lyndsey Oliver

David O'Neill
Clare Owen
Philiy Page
David Park
Nick Parker
– The CancerJourneyMan
Danny Parr
Doc Parsons
Carlotta Pasquinelli
Ilaria Pasquinelli
Sarah Patton
Paula
Nick Pennell
Garrett Pitcher
Simon Platt
Sarah Potter
Robert Poynton
Damian Pratt
Tom Pratt
Lesley Preece
Kirsten Proctor
David Punchard
Donagh Quigley
Patrick Quinn
India Rabey
Toby Ramsden Clark
Babet Reinders
Keith Richards
Craig Richardson
Lesley Richardson
Catherine Ritchie
Savannah Roach
Neil Robinson
Kevin Roche
Lucia Rolli
Joris Roovers
Johannes Romppanen
Charles Ross
Nigel Rushman
Pedro Russo
Suzanne Russo
Leo Ryan
Edd Salter
Ian Sanders
Catherine Sarsfield
Jonathan Satchell
Peter Saunders, OBE
Dan Scott
Anant Sharma
Marie Sheel
Chris Shepard

Stewart Sheppard
Stephen Sowden-Mabbott
Matt Spry
Benedict Steele
Sophie Stephenson
Eric Stevens
Jon Stewart
Ruben Stragier
Nick Stratford
Pete Stuart
Duke Stump
& Molly Supple
Kinan Suchaovanich
Mark Summers
Jo Tait
James Taplin
Greg Taylor
Marcus Taylor
Inês Teles Correia
Paul Thomas
Rowland Thomas
Guy Thompson
Tomo Thompson
Louisa Thomsen Brits
Philip Tidy
Owen Turner
Paul Turner
Stephen Turner
U + I
Upcott Farm
Frank Van Damme
Petra van den Houten
Melanie Vanderhei
Selfa Verlaat
Vincent Viala
Andra Vlaicu
Mark Warman
Irfon Watkins
Wanda Weller
Keir Whitaker
Tor White
Andrew Wilkie
Neil Williams
Huw Wilson
Julie Wilson
Tom Wood
Ross Worby
Simon & Maryann Wright
Richard Young

Picture credits

The publisher and the Do Lectures would like to thank the following talented photographers for their contribution to this book. Some were commissioned exclusively by the Do Lectures to capture the event and speakers.

All images in the book with the exception of those detailed below © Jim Marsden

Pages:

34, 129 © Richard Beaven
60, 68, 215 and speaker portraits Do Wales 2008—2010 © James Bowden
10, 142, 178 © Peter Castagnetti and Barret Bowman
62, 64, 66, 70, 76, 205, 242 and speaker portraits 2011—2013 © Jonathan Cherry
231 © Libby Delana
9 © Tom Dolman
127 © Anja Dunk
209 © Simon Edwards
118, 140, 141, 146, 147, 148, 162, 232, 237 © Sue Fan and Danielle Quigley
28, 93, 118, 149, 150 © Nick Hand
298 © David Hieatt
74, 187, 207, 240 and speaker portraits for Do USA 2016 © Winky Lewis
59 © Benjamin Lennox
Speaker portraits for Do Australia 2014 and 2015 © Mark Lobo
42 © Dan Mace
281, 287, 292 and speaker portraits for Do USA 2013 © Michael Piazza
174 (bottom) and speaker portraits for Do USA 2015 © Helena Price
294, 296 © Dan Rubin
79 © Mickey Smith
211 © James Taplin
30, 31, 61, 63, 81 and speaker portraits for Do USA 2014 © Jesse Webster
229 © Paige Wright
228 © Magdalena Wosinska

Further reading

The following Do publications are also available:

Do Books

Do Beekeeping
The secret to happy
honeybees
Orren Fox

Do Birth
A gentle guide to labour
and childbirth
Caroline Flint

Do Breathe
Calm your mind. Find focus.
Get stuff done
Michael Townsend Williams

Do Design
Why beauty is key to
everything
Alan Moore

Do Disrupt
Change the status quo.
Or become it
Mark Shayler

Do Fly
Find your way. Make a
living. Be your best self
Gavin Strange

Do Grow
Start with 10 simple
vegetables
Alice Holden

Do Improvise
Less push. More pause.
Better results. A new
approach to work (and life)
Robert Poynton

Do Inhabit
Style your space for a
creative and considered life
Sue Fan, Danielle Quigley

Do Lead
Share your vision.
Inspire others.
Achieve the impossible
Les McKeown

Do Listen
Understand what's really
being said. Find a new way
forward
Bobette Buster

Do Open
How a simple email
newsletter can transform
your business (and it can)
David Hieatt

Do Preserve
Make your own jams,
chutneys, pickles and
cordials
Anja Dunk, Jen Goss,
Mimi Beaven

Do Protect
Legal advice for startups
Johnathan Rees

Do Purpose
Why brands with a purpose
do better and matter more
David Hieatt

Do Sourdough
Slow bread for busy lives
Andrew Whitley

Do Story
How to tell your story so
the world listens
Bobette Buster

Do Wild Baking
Food, fire and good times
Tom Herbert

Do Inspirationals

Path
A short story about
reciprocity
Louisa Thomsen Brits

The Skimming Stone
A short story about courage
Dominic Wilcox

The Path of a Doer
A simple tale on how to get
things done
David Hieatt

Available in print and digital
formats from bookshops,
online retailers or via our
website: thedobook.co

Do Reports

The Side Project Report

The Stress Report

Available in print format via:
thedolectures.com

To find out more about
our company, books and
authors, please visit
thedobook.co or follow us
@dobookco

You can find the Do Lectures
@thedolectures. If you are
interested in watching any of
the talks online or attending
the event, please visit:
thedolectures.com

It's not often you can pinpoint an exact moment when life changed, but here is a picture of one of those rare gifts. Four years ago I went to a little festival in Wales where it pissed with rain and my heart broke open so wide, I knew life would never be the same. And indeed it wasn't. These past four years have seen some pretty epic shit go down and all of it because of this one long weekend in Wales at @The Do Lectures. Thank you a million times and a million times again for all that has happened for me. It changed my life, actually it saved it 🤍🙏🤍